NORTHERN
FOLK 2

First Published in England in the United Kingdom
In the year 2003
Bermac Publications Newton Aycliffe,
www.bermac.co.uk
E/Mail bernie@bermac.co.uk
Tel. 01325-311956

ISBN 0-9541756-1-1

Typeset in 11pt Times New Roman
Titles in 18pt Times New Roman
Typesetting and originating by
Bermac Publications.
Printed and Bound in Great Britain
BY MACDONALD PRESS LIMITED, TUDHOE.

Front Cover '*Cragside*', Northumberland; ex home of Lord William Armstrong
Portraits of Sir Joseph Swan & Sir Charles Parsons

Bibliography

Robert Surtees	Autobiography
Charles Swan	George Hunter(1852)
A Private View of L.S. Lowry	Shelley Rohde(1979)
Stories of Great Explorers	Leonard Gribble
Great Engineers	John Merrett
Journey through the History of Middlesbrough	Norman Moorsom
Charles Parsons	Rollo Appleyard
Lives of the Engineers	Samuel Smiles
The Eddystone Lighthouse(london 1882)	E. P. Edwards
British Lighthouses (London 1913)	J.S. Wryde
A History of Lighthouses	Patrick Beaver
History of Durham	Robert Surtees
The Durham Directory	

Every effort has been made to contact copy right holders of any material reproduced in the book; any omissions will be rectified in further printing if notice is given to the publisher.

This book is dedicated to my late parents Jane Fletcher & Michael McCormick sadly missed:

FORWORD

The North of England is steeped in History and achievements of Engineers, Authors, Scientists who all made major Improvements to our Industrial Heritage; creating wealth and prosperity of, not only the North of England; but also Great Britain and the rest of the world.

After the publication of 'Northern Folk in 2000, and noting the interest in the book I realized that the north of England was still brimming with notable characters that contributed so much to the present well being of England and the rest of the world. Charles Parson discovered the turbine that revolutionized engines and ocean going liners; putting this country ahead of rivals. In the beginning of the 18th. Century our country relied on coal to produce power, work and hard earned currency from abroad so that we could feed our young families. William Coulson and his men sank over a hundred Collieries boring into an abundance of much needed coal. John Harrison with his accurate maritime clock made shipping easier and safer. Elliott Verdon Roe, and Sir Joseph Swan were leaders in aviation and incandescent lighting; Joseph Whitworth, John Smeaton and Bolckow and Vaughan, were specialists in their particular fields, all were very necessary for the progress of our country. William Wilberforce was a brilliant politician who changed the law to free slaves. Robert Surtees wrote the 'History of Durham', and L.S. Lowry completed unusual art that is now worth thousands of pounds; and much sought after. In conclusion George Hudson was an amazing man who developed the railways in England. Altogether there are twelve characters, they all, make compelling reading, and I spent many pleasant hours researching and writing about these dynamic people.

Most Autobiographies and information on these brilliant people are long out of date and information on them is hard to come by; schools when teaching History seem only to go as far back as the First World War; making it more important to keep the lives of these amazing pioneers at hand and I have strived to make details on their lives available, by researching and writing 12 further short Biographies on them.

It is only right and proper because of their major contributions and achievements that they all should be remembered and honoured.

LIST OF CONTENTS

Select Bibliography
Forward

CHARLES ALGERNON PARSONS
(Discovered turbine engines)

It did not take much thought to include Charles Parsons in my book *Northern Folk 2*. Charles Parson is a part of the North of England even though being born in London. He completed his life's work in and around Tyneside, inventing the Turbine Engine and testing it successfully on the Turbinia. Parsons also completed his apprenticeship with another northern legend, William Armstrong Whitworth & Company. Finally, ask any *'Geordie'*, whom he most admired in the area or who he would most recommend his son to work for as an apprentice, and he will undoubtedly say Charles Parsons. Being greatly admired in the North East.

Charles Parsons was born June 13th, 1854, at 13, Connaught Place, Hyde Park, London. This happens to be at the junction where Edgware Road and Bayswater Road, meet at Tyburn. His father was Lord Rosse [6th *Baronet, 3rd Earl of Rosse]* and it was from this address in 1854 that he sent a letter to Sir John Burgoyne, who was then Chief of the Engineering Department of the British Army, saying it was his dream to build an iron Steamer, proof against shot, shells or boarders, that could run at the enemy ships sinking them with one blow above the cut water. Three in one plate would be used, and the funnel would not appear above the deck. It was assumed that a 300hp engine would be required to power the ship. It would take Charles Parsons thirty years to start to realize his father's dream, by first of all solving the propulsion method of such ships, and in the process find other discoveries that would greatly improve existence for the human race.

Birr Castle was the family home at Parsons Town, Ireland. Charles had five brothers all had advantages that other people would envy. Their father was a Member of Parliament and also president of The Royal Society, *[a post that many scientists longed for]*. The months of May and June were always spent in London, going to their grandmothers at Brighton in July, then returning to Ireland

6

in the autumn. A fire destroyed the central part of Birr Castle. After restoration the Castle retained its wall thickness, and a forge and workshop were constructed in the old moat. A furnace was also added to melt brass. Another addition was an engine house with machinery for polishing specula for telescopes. There were also lathes for wood and ironwork. Every kind of repair was possible. This is where Charles and his father spent all their spare time when Charles was a boy; many achievements and problems were solved here. Basically, they had an open-air life, rowing fishing and shooting. Lessons were 7.30am breakfast 8am, lessons 9am to noon. They were out of doors until lunch at 2pm, lessons again from 5pm till 6.30. During these days in Ireland there was much unrest, murders, and robberies were not uncommon. Their father often went to his observatory and astronomical telescope with pistols in his belt. All shrubs were cut down so as to not to create cover for anyone. But the family was always left alone.

Prince Albert consulted Lord Rosse, often; Canon Randal Parsons said Laurence often played with the Royal children. Queen Victoria held Lord Rosse in high esteem and when he died wrote a letter in her own hand of gracious sympathy to the Countess. Sir Robert Ball described Birr Castle:

'It was a noble place surrounded by a moat, situated in a park through which flowed two rivers, that there unite, about the Lake which was made by Lord Rosse, 'The waters of the lake operated a water wheel to drain the low lying lands. The telescope was supported by two parallel walls, situated between Birr Castle and the Lake, the tube of the Newtonian, sixty feet long and more than six feet across carried at its lower end the mirror and at the top the eyepiece'.

The observer needed four assistants to adjust the mechanism to his needs.

During any spare time, Charles could be seen in the workshop making all kinds of machines – which were all used effectively. One of the machines, which Charles made, was a steam engine. Another successful job he did was to grind the reflector of a telescope.

The brothers began to keep a twenty-ton yacht at Ryde, Cowes, and sometimes at Southampton, It wintered at Leamington or Dublin. They then bought *'Themia'*, an iron yacht, which was 150 tons. The brothers crossed the English Channel in her; they also visited Cherbourg, via. Lands end, prior to visiting Ireland. They then purchased *'Titania'*, which was 188 tons and also iron, but very fast. *'Titania'*, had belonged to Robert Stephenson, the son of the famous engineer George Stephenson. She drew fourteen feet of water, was fitted with a large balloon jib, and balloon topsails for racing. They cruised in her from Dublin to Stornoway, Cape Wrath, and Wick, then to the east coast of England. They also cruised to Belgium and Holland and Amsterdam, the Zuider Zee off Germany. They also visited the workshops of the diamond cutters. Rochelle and along the Spanish coast was also visited. In 1867 they made a tour of Cologne,

Basle and Geneva. This ended the family holidays, because sadly their father died. After the death of Lord Rosse they stayed at the Castle a further year, then they took a house in Dublin, first at Raglan Road then at Merrion Road. They still managed to have their summer holidays in 1868 and 1869 at the Castle. Charles began Trinity College, Dublin, with his brother Clere. Their father had been Chancellor here so it was fitting that Charles and his brother should study here. He did very well, winning prizes for mathematics and German language. Charles proceeded to Cambridge where he excelled again in mathematics. While Charles was in College he was an excellent rower, he competed for whichever College he was studying in at the time. Charles Parsons went from Cambridge to Elswick, Newcastle upon Tyne. He had gained a distinction in Mathematics, and he came to Newcastle to further his career, doing a three-year apprenticeship at the famous Armstrong Whitworth Works. It was his intention to enquire further into Electro Magnetic engines.

During Parsons boyhood Lupus developed the Torpedo. In 1870 the Whitehead Torpedo had carried 18 pounds of dynamite. The Admiralty was interested in this project and they bought it for £15,000. In 1872 the famous Peter Brotherhood engine for driving torpedoes appeared. This impressed Parsons immensely stimulating him into producing an Epicycloidal engine and a steam turbine. From 1877 to 1884 his research in this area kept him fully occupied. Parsons built an experimental engine. It was a compound engine, with four cylinders revolving at half speed on the crankshaft. He applied it to drive a Siemans dynamo, at 7000 revolutions a minute. It was 10hp, and for a time supplied the arc light at Elswick jetty. The engine had continuous lubrication by a pump; he also fitted a frictional spring clutch drive. The engine was put to work in a Millwright shop at an ordinance works. Later an Erith firm used the engine and it was so satisfactory for their needs they made more, with good results. By now Charles Parsons had finished his apprenticeship at Armstrong's works and the following letter was sent from the works and endorsed by William Armstrong himself.

'Elswick Works,
Newcastle Upon Tyne,
June 3rd. 1881
The Hon. C.A. Parsons,
Dear Sir,
In reply to your request for a recommendation from our firm to assist you in your search for a partnership in an Engineering establishment, pray make use of this letter in which we have pleasure of bearing testimony to your high theoretical knowledge, your constructive abilities, and your promising business

qualifications. With this letter we hand you your indentures, which you will observe Sir William Armstrong has kindly certified. We are Sir
Yours faithfully
WG. Armstrong & Co.

At this time his thoughts were constantly on Turbines, rockets and torpedoes, it was also on marriage.... He met his future wife, Katherine Bethell, in 1882. Katherine was pretty good at needlework and Charles also got very interested and soon he found ways to do it better than Katherine. It was just amazing, how easily he could learn to master any problem in no time at all.

The marriage between Charles and Katherine took place on January 10th 1883, in the Church of All saints in Bramham, Yorkshire. The rector was William Whatley, Rector of Rise and Canon of York. Their first home was in lodgings in Leeds. Parsons was so absorbed in the design of torpedoes; during his honeymoon he took his bride and also a mechanic to trials, early every morning. They arrived daily in bitter cold and frosty weather at 7am. It was during these cold mornings that Katherine caught rheumatic fever. By the spring of 1884 she had fully recovered and they resumed their honeymoon, this time in a warmer environment, and it lasted for five months. They visited America, New Mexico and California. They stayed in a small boarding house in Los-Angeles; and also visited Pittsburgh, Chicago. In Chicago, as if Katherine hadn't suffered enough, she was attacked by one of a herd of cattle and she was pinned between its wide horns. Shortly after this they returned happily home. He now joined Clark & Chapman & Co. of Gateshead as a junior partner and for a while studied electric lighting and steam turbines instead of torpedoes. He soon discovered that with a suitable dynamo, the turbine would serve for electric lighting of ships. Charles Parsons wrote the following in his own writing and words in 1884

In the year 1884, circumstances being favourable, I was determined to attack the problem of steam turbines and of a very high-speed dynamo and alternator to be directly driven by it. The efficiency of this dynamo was about 80% and the steam consumption of the plant about 150 lbs. Per kilowatt-hour. This little turbo worked satisfactorily from the start.

Charles and Katherine started to turn their attention to a suitable home. Initially they decided on a house in Corbridge on Tyne. This meant that Charles had to leave for Gateshead at 7.30am returning at 8pm. This proved impossible to carry on and within a year they made their home at Elvaston Hall, Ryton on Tyne, Durham.

Rachel Mary Parsons was born January 25th, 1885, and on October 19th1886, their son, Algernon George, was born – both at Elvaston Hall. They stayed happily here for ten years. Their homes at the time were extraordinary;

9

machines were made out of anything, cotton reels and old drums. The Ryton home was lit by arc lamps, incandescent lamps not yet having been invented. Parsons looked for new ways to wind dynamos. From the home workshop, with his daughter Rachel by his side, he produced all kinds of toys. There was the 'Spider', a small engine with spirit fuel (it had three wheels, two small and one large). This travelled around the garden and lawn with the dogs chasing it. There was also a steam pram for carrying the children, and a small flying machine was also constructed. This had again spirit as a fuel and was actually photographed in full flight, showing that Charles had a lot of faith in aviation as early as this.

During his early-married life Charles and his wife visited Connaught Place, where his mother Mary Lady Rosse talked about Charles's boyhood saying that he would not contemplate 'eating without having his bricks and mechanical toys with him

This man would be a boy again, and be a father too...

The serious side of his work was rapidly developing. In 1885 his first steam turbine was running successfully at Gateshead. Six horsepower at 18000 revolutions a minute. The Chilean battleship *'Blanco Encalada'* arrived at Elswick for new boilers and armaments. This was the first warship to be fitted with a Parsons Turbine & Dynamos-set for electric lighting. By the time Charles Parsons was thirty years of age he was well on his way to a successful engineering career. In 1885 while at Gateshead, Clark Chapman and Co. fitted the ill-fated HMS *'Victoria'* with one of Parsons 12 kilowatt combined turbo generators, No.13. In May 1887 Parsons was making 4 Kilowatt 'sets', for the Suez Canal and he was also completing similar contracts for the Italian, Spanish and Chilean Navies. His turbines were rapidly being improved and the relationship of the velocity of the steam, to the velocity of the blades received careful attention to improve the efficiency. During 1884-1885 two small portable turbine sets were completed at Gateshead. In January 1886 there was a severe frost and the swan pond near Sheriff Hill was frozen hard. The Chief Constable of Gateshead, Mr. Elliott suggested that if the pond could be illuminated, skaters could be attracted charging them a small fee for admission; some cash could be raised for the local Hospital. Clark and Parsons gladly lent the portable set, and RN. Redmane in the Newcastle Evening Chronicle of July 22 1931 described the occasion.

Elliott carted the Turbine up to the ground, where it was set up. Lamps were hung round the pond, and the Turbine was got to work. Mr. Joseph Swan supplied the lamps. It was a great success from Elliot's point of view, because the place was so crowded, that few people could really skate. But every one paid to get in, to say that they had actually skated by electric light. As far as I can

' remember the frost lasted three days and the Royal Infirmary benefited by £100'

In 1887 Parsons became known as the designer of Plant for the generation of Electricity. In that particular year, ten of his Turbo Generators, from 15 Kilowatts to 32 Kilowatts each, supplied most of the current lighting for the Newcastle Exhibition – by means of incandescent lamps. The turbo generator being made at Clark Chapman & Parsons at Gateshead on Tyne. This was reported to be the most efficient exhibition of incandescent lighting held at the time.

These were exciting days for Charles Parsons, he established the suitability of his Turbo-Alternator for town electricity supply he also built machines for Newcastle District Electric Lighting Company and it was mainly due to this wonderful period that Charles Parsons won the freedom of the City of Newcastle upon Tyne in 1914. When Charles and his friend, Dr. John Bell Simpson, were out shooting, he mentioned to Parsons, why he did not try his turbines to drive ships, to which Charles replied 'the time was ripe for the attempt'.

In 1889 the Partnership of Clarke, Chapman & Co. was dissolved. Parsons established a works at Heaton, near Newcastle to manufacture steam turbines for use on land; they also manufactured high-speed electrical machinery suitable for coupling straight to turbines. The works covered two acres. The main shop being 170 feet long and 50 feet wide. There was also a blacksmiths shop, testing rooms and offices. At the time the total staff was 48. This was a sharp contrast to the works in 1931 when C.A. Parsons & Co. Ltd. of Heaton covered 20 acres and employed 2000 people. His main erecting bay measured 416 feet long and 50 feet wide. During 1895, Westing House Machinery Company, acquired the American rights, for installations on land in America. Messrs. Brown & Boveri, to enable the Parsons Turbine to be built in America, mainly for Europe, obtained licences in 1901.

The Parsons name was certainty expanding. There were however downturns as well. At one of the land stations in Shanghai, in November 1923, there was a terrible accident with a 20,000-kilowatt turbo alternator. At the time it was running unloaded at moderate speed. The turbine rotor shaft forging burst and some lives were lost. There had been a concealed defect in the interior of the forging. The shaft had been made in 1921 from a cold ingot of medium carbon steel of unknown history. An independent company, who accepted responsibility for the defect, had manufactured it. *[The defect was possibly a 'clink', an internal crack arising from the too rapid heating of the metal during the forging]* News of the disaster came when Parsons was attending a dinner in London of the 'British Electrical & Allied Manufacturers Association'. Parsons was dining with fellow directors and had to sit right through dinner knowing about the accident.

11

They convened a Board meeting at midnight the same evening. At·this meeting it was decided to cable Shanghai accepting responsibility. The exact wording for the cable was as follows.

"Deepest regrets at serious accident and loss of life. Sending immediately 2 chief experts to investigate. Keep all parts for evidence. Will replace turbine and recondition the whole of your plant, entirely at our cost!"

Another setback was an explosion aboard *'King George V'*, on September 29th. 1927, two ship's firemen lost their lives. This greatly distressed Parsons. The cause, after some time, was traced to scale in the water. Later it was decided only to use distilled water in these high-pressure water boilers. The ship, after rectification, resumed with satisfactory results.

After Charles Parsons parted company with Clarke Chapman & Co. He received the £20,000, which he had initially put in the company. With his patents for the turbines it was a little more difficult. For some years there was arbitration and litigation, it all stemmed from an agreement on individual patents taken out when a board of director resigned his directorship. These became the property of the Company. When Charles tried to regain these, he found that he would have to pay a very large sum, being the present day value of the patent. It did not seem quite right that he would have to pay Chapman and Clarke an inflated amount of cash just to work his own patents. Parsons decided to fight the action, which had been endorsed by the arbitrators. There was another point raised at the time, which was that the patents would be virtually useless without Parson himself. Litigation continued for years until it was decided that 'Clarke Chapman & Company' carry on with Parsons patents without Parsons; in effect develop them on their own. Parsons carried on with his turbines using a different design than the original. As for Clarke and Chapman, although holding the patents they never made any money out of them – not without Charles Parsons! Later, Parsons, through efforts of Camble and Swinton, was able to regain the patents for a very moderate amount.

Turbinia

Charles Parsons began to look further into his turbines possibly being used in ocean going shipping, which included warships. The advantages of Marine Propulsion were summarized.

1 *Increased Speed,*
2 *Increased carrying power of vessel*
3 *Increased economies in steam consumption*
4 *Increased facilities for navigation of shallow waters*
5 *Reduced initial costs*
6 *Reduced weight of Machinery*
7 *Reduced cost of attendance on machinery*

8 Diminished cost of upkeep of machinery
9 Largely reduced vibration
10 Reduce size and weight of screw propellers and shafting.

Parsons had to prove these claims and they decided to construct an experimental vessel 100 feet in length, to be propelled by a turbine of 1000hp, for this purpose they built the *'Turbinia'*,

In 1897 a new Company was formed 'The Parsons Marine Steam Turbine Company'. It had a registered capital of £500,000 divided into 5000 shares, each of £100 with a first issue of £240,000. The original Company transferred to this company all its powers under the 'Parsons patents'. It took over the right to any future extension or improvements. The prospectus added: **'...it is proposed forthwith to acquire the advantages of a site on the Tyne for manufacturing turbines and the equipment of Torpedo Boats, Destroyers, and vessels generally. The technical management of the undertaking will remain with Mr. Parsons as Managing Director.'**

The *'Turbinia'* to date had 31 trials at full speed. Single, two bladed, single four bladed multiple treble propellers, with every modification fitted, the best results were obtained with treble props. twenty-two inches in diameter. Which at 1780 revolutions gave Turbinia *19,3/4,* knots. It was an advance but it could do better and more experiments were needed. Gerald Stoney who took part in early trials with the *Turbinia'* said its reverse gear was imperfect. On one occasion they tried to turn about in the Tyne, they reached the side of the river but owing to the current they could not go further round, and they collided with a cargo steamer, *'The North Tyne'*. The *'Turbinia's'*, sharp bow made a hole in the side of the ship, this being eighteen inches long. Parson's and the crew did well with boat hooks, but the collision could not be avoided. *'North Tyne'*, put into dock for a new plate. One other occasion, Lady Parsons and Miss Rachel were on board, the skipper sighted one of Armstrong's 23-knot vessels off the Tyne. On board the *'Turbinia'*, they closed the hatches. Accelerating to 28 knots, they overtook the vessel, leaving her far astern. She responded by a friendly blast from her whistle. One of the officers from Armstrong's boat said that all they saw when the *'Turbinia'*, went past was a big wave, with a black bow emerging and a flame of fire shooting out from the middle. The bow wave of the *'Turbinia'*, swept the deck and all on board were drenched, including Miss Rachel, who stepped down into the forward stokehold to dry off with her brother. The Turbine engines of the *'Turbinia'* were built at Heaton, and Heaton must be recognized as the place of the birth of Parsons Turbine's. The turbines for *'HMS Viper'*, and *'Cobra'*, were made at Wallsend. On suitable days measured mile trials were carried out at sea. Some observers were from the Admiralty and these were described as 'thorough sport', at 32 knots in the open sea, all the ladies on board expected, and got a soaking. There was a great deal of French interest in the *'Turbinia'*, and in 1900 the boat was an important item of the Paris exhibition. Arrangements were made to have speed runs on a wide part of the river Seine. She was taken there the day before the trial. The French Minister of Marine was there and small steamers from Rouen formed a lane, in which *'Turbinia'*, sped, and the crowds cheered loudly. Later she proceeded to Havre. In the distance the Newhaven-Dieppe, steamer was travelling towards England, *'Turbinia'*, easily caught up with her and made circles round her, she finally broke off and steered to Grimsby, then the Tyne. The Paris trip took three weeks. The *'Turbinia'*, did really well on trials and it prompted Parsons to start to look for expansion. Land rents varied from £50 to £70 per acre, while freehold was £1000-£1500 an acre. It was predicted also at the time, that the *'Turbinia'*, would reach speeds of 33-34 knots.

HMS Cobra – HMS Viper:

With the success of *'Turbinia*, two further vessels were constructed and both would end in disaster. These were *'Cobra'* & *'Viper'*, on August the 3rd 1901 HMS *'Viper'*, fitted with Parsons turbines, floundered on Renouquet Island, near Alderney, and was a total wreck. On September 18th 1901, HMS *'Cobra'*, fitted out exactly the same as its sister ship, broke in two off the Outer Dowsing Shoal, on the Lincolnshire coast. She was being navigated from the Tyne to Portsmouth. The whole world was awaiting the trials of these vessels after the successes of the *'Turbinia'*. There were many enquiries regarding the two ships and in December 1905 Parsons gave a lecture at Armstrong College, Newcastle when he said that although the *'Viper'* & *'Cobra'*, were lost through no fault of the turbines, it was apparent that the whole system was in danger of collapsing. It was on this account that the turbine Company was formed. This directly led to the building of the first turbine propelled merchant vessel, the *'King Edward'*, in the spring of 1900. After the *'Turbinia'*, and its sister ships it was well known what Tyneside could do to provide propulsion for war vessels. Nearly every Navy, in the World, adopted Parsons' turbines. By 1909 Parsons had provided turbines in warships of some million-horse power, merchant shipping probably half that amount. The speed required by Navy's averaged 25 knots. The Royal Navy required even faster ships than this and it was not achievable without Parsons' turbines. In 1906 the first turbine driven capital ship was HMS *'Dreadnought'*, that year Cunard got *'Lusitania'*, and *'Mauritania'*, fitted with 70,000 hp. Turbines. The Royal Navy ordered battle ships like *'Dreadnought'*, *'Invincible'*, *'Inflexible'*, *'Indomitable'*, in 1908, 1909 & speed of 26 knots, later *'HMS. Hood'* by John Brown and Co. propelled by turbines of 150,000hp, had speeds of 32 knots. Later, the Falkland crisis demonstrated just how important Parsons' turbines were on warships. Because of England's stand against German domination in two world wars it was inevitable that some of Parsons' turbine fitted ships would come under attack, two of these were *"Lusitania"* and *"HMS Hood"*, and the following are the accounts of the terrible loss of life that was sustained.

"Lusitania"

Beautiful four funnel British steam ship of the Cunard line, was torpedoed without warning during the 14/18 war by a German submarine on May 7th 1915, off the southern coast of Ireland. The ship sank in 20 minutes with the loss of 1198 persons including 128 Americans. The Germans said that the ship was carrying arms, [later proved true) and that the Americans had been warned against taking passage on a British vessel in a notice that had appeared in an American newspaper on the day that the ship had sailed from New York. This sinking angered the American people and the ill feeling against Germany was overwhelming, there was pressure on the American government to declare war on Germany. President Woodrow Wilson chose a diplomatic course, sending the German Foreign Secretary three successive notes, demanding that Germany disavow the sinking and make reparations. Germany refused to accept responsibility for the tragedy but did agree to make reparations and to sink no more passenger ships without warning.

Walter Schwieger, the U20 submarine captain had other ideas and defied his superiors orders, by sinking the 'Hesperian', on 4th September, 1915, then sinking a further five more steamers all in the course of three days; 'Druro', 'Rea', 'Dictator', 'Bordeaux', 'Caroni'. Walter Schwieger himself, shared the same fate on 5th September 1917 when striking an allied mine while on his way to again, cause havoc for allied shipping, this disregard for discipline eventually went a long way to lose both wars for Germany. Captain Turner who had commanded most of Cunard's fleet of steamers commanded the Lusitania. A German submarine also sank 'Ivernia', which was under Turner's command on New Years Day, 1917, off Cape Mapatan, Greece.

'H.M.S Hood'

The Hood was initially engaged in the Atlantic, then in the Mediterranean, taking part in the Mers-el-Kebir Affair. The ship at the time was as long as the best Japanese ship Yamoto, 262 m., this was longer than the Bismarck, which was 251 m. The speed of the Hood was 30 knots, faster than the Yamoto, which had 27 knots, Bismarck being faster than the two with 32 knots

H.M.S. Hood was sadly sunk on 24th. May 1941, by the German pocket Battleship, 'Bismarck'. The Hood had put to sea, with 1253 men on board, of these 86 were officers. The ship, thank God, was under manned, at the time being capable of carrying 1420 men. There was 3 survivors, all 3 received mentioned in dispatches. The author's brother in law [Charles Bartlett] had been due to sail with Hood on the day of the sailing but was ill in Hospital. The Bismarck shared

15

a similar fate when a Swordfish launched from Ark Royal hit the Bismarck's rudder with a lucky torpedo in May 1941, in the north Atlantic. She was finished off by gunfire; sinking in 30 minutes. Most of the 2200 crew perished apart from 115, who were saved. Ark Royal was sunk by Nazi Sub. U-81 after returning from delivering Hurricane fighters to besieged Malta and was the third in line to bear that name. The first fought the Spanish Armada in 1588 the current one is the fifth in line and will lead the present possible assault against Iraq. The amazing fact about the wartime sinking of Ark Royal, only one sailor *(E. Mitchell)* died, the rest of the 1,500 crew were saved by other ships. 30 miles off Gibraltar on November 13th. 1941

Sound Reproducers and Extreme Mine Sinking

Parsons interests were not confined to only turbines; he was interested in everything and anything. In 1906, two trumpet shaped objects appeared at the Queens Hall, London. These were for increasing the volume and richness of tone, mainly of stringed instruments, and they were on trial at the hall. Auxetophone-gramaphone concerts were given in towns throughout the country as well as in Australia and New Zealand. By 1909 the fame of the Auxetophone had increased. Musicians, and especially Sir Henry Wood, received it very well. Charles Parsons had earlier taken out patents in various sound recorders which improved over the years from the initial gramophone recorders. In one of the earlier types of Auxeto phone, the gramophone needle was fixed into a socket formed integrally with the valve cover. The needle ran in the groove on the face of the 'record' disc. Parsons used the Edison counter-weight lever and sapphire stylus for picking up and transmitting sound waves

Deep Mining

Parsons was bent upon digging a mile below the earth strata, where unknown treasures may be waiting to be disturbed. One reason for his idea of extreme mining was that it could yield oil and coal that could not have been envisaged from moderate depth mines. Parsons consulted Mr. John Bell Simpson, the eminent authority of the times on mining, in the North of England. The shaft would be sunk in stages each about half a mile in depth; even haulage and machinery were considered at each stage. It was estimated that at the time it would cost £5,000,000 to bore to a depth of 12 miles. Parsons took a long look concerning the validity of the project and it was said at the time, by Simpson his consultant, *"that beneath our feet are unexplored coalfields"*. **He went on to** say that, *"it would be most interesting Geological investigation of National and Commercial importance; if workable seams at moderate depths could be proved it would add another 200 years to the Great Northern coalfields"*.

In the first instance, boreholes would throw a considerable light on the subject and it would be inexpensive. The 'creep' was at this time discussed by them in mine levels where the rock not only bulges in from above but also rises up from below. It is known from most deep workings and in the case of deep boreholes; a cylinder of rock of the section of the bore gradually rises, it is a matter of surprise that the rock in deep gorges does not tend to creep in and close the gully.

Parsons visited the Geothermal Power Plant of Larderrello, which was operated by the steam springs of Tuscany on the extreme northern border of Maremma. Prince Ginori-Conti described the plant in July 1924, during the world power conference at Wembley. The Prince explained that these natural jets emit only steam, thereby differing from ordinary geysers that release steam and water. The name of these is 'Saffoni', and an engine successfully ran for 15 years from this steam. Later 3 generating units were added using turbines. At a meeting of the 'Royal Society', at the time, Sir Charles proposed that the earth's natural heat should be utilized by drilling a well of sufficient depth to reach high temperatures. The Prince said that Parsons idea had been implimented in their system in his country and was very effective.

Optical Glass

It is understandable that Parsons should be interested in Astronomy and products related lenses for searchlights and astronomy equipment. In 1882 Dr Schott joined forces with Abbe who lived at Jena, they also became associated with Carl Zeiss (1816-1888). Carl was the son of a toy proprietor, but since 1846 made scientific instruments in a factory at Jena. They came together to form a Company for this business.

Schott and Abbe began experimenting on the improvements of lenses to obtain sharper definition, equal central and marginal magnification and absence of colour fringes, this together with a maximum intensity of transmitted light. The activities at Jena during the World War 1, was amazing, they employed more than 10,000 people, 50% of these woman. After the war, the numbers employed dropped to about 5,000. The industry in England caused Parsons much anxiety as he saw England dropping behind more experienced countries in the manufacture of optical glass. It had been estimated that Jena products prior to 1914 produced about 60% of the Worlds' optical glass; Paris 30%, Birmingham the remainder. Between 1917-1918, Wood Brothers Glass Company of Barnsley was asked to supply optical glass for the War Office and the Admiralty and the Ministry for Munitions – an amount of 1000 lbs a month. The order was then increased to 1500 lbs. They also had to have a reserve stock of 7500 lbs.

After 1920 the industry was imperiled and it looked like certain collapse. Parson intervened acquired the shares, paid off all of the creditors, and allowed funds for cash flow, so that the Company could continue. Charles knew he would have no financial gain whatsoever, but he was determined to save the company, as he knew that the industry was necessary for the scientific and industrial welfare of his Country. By June 30th 1929, the capital contributed by him for the project was £57,000. Later England perfected the art of optical glass manufacture and due to his perseverance, when all seemed lost, this industry was able to hold its own. Because of his father's interest in astronomy and his own interest in lenses Parsons was able to foresee this problem, and with his financial strength at the time, was able to avert a very serious catastrophe for England.

Parsons the Man

Parsons never ever had one day of poverty in his life, he was born an aristocrat. In his business life he always had plenty of willing helpers. He was always a very strong man. When he could he always cycled to work. He then drove his car, which had to be cranked to start, it needed strength to do this. He was fined £5 with £1 costs for speeding, and not producing his licence. He rarely consulted a doctor but for others he would insist on the best specialists possible and any aids to make life tolerable. He could design anything and his knowledge was immense. More time was spent at his works office than anywhere. He was especially proud of the *'Turbinia'*. He was slightly deaf and at times seemed deep in thought, but any visitors received a warm overwhelming welcome.

Parsons always considered the future not the past. On November 6th, 1902, he received from Sir Michael Foster, the secretary of the Royal Society, the 'Rumford medal' for his invention of the Turbine and extension into Navigation. On March 5th, 1910, when he lived at Holeyn Hall, Wylam on Tyne, he was nominated and appointed Sheriff of the County of Northumberland. He was required 'to take Custody and charge, of the said County during his Majesty's pleasure'. On June 10th, 1911, he was honoured with a Knight Commander of the Bath, just prior to the Coronation. On September 13th 1915, he was made Chairman of the Tyne & Wear board of Management under the Ministry of Munitions.

Parsons was a keen fisherman when staying in Scotland, with Mr. Norman Cookson; he shot a stag, and on the same day bagged 4 salmon. He enjoyed trout fishing either in Lochs or rivers; he always remembered that his best catch was at Lord Armstrong's home. They were catching one after the other forgetting that it was the first day of September, a water bailiff approached them telling them he was confiscating the fish and their rods as they were fishing against the law, in fact they were a day too late. Lord Armstrong intervened and the bailiff let them go. All the time Lady Armstrong waited to cook the trout, which did not arrive.

Charles Parsons had a welcome visitor to his garden at Holeyn Hall, it was a sulphur-crested cockatoo, and it seemed to come from nowhere and stayed 35 years. As a reader he enjoyed a thrilling novel and always remembered Dickens and Kipling. Like everyone else he had downturns in life. When he

18

heard about the *'Cobra'*, disaster, he locked himself in his office and stayed there all day long. 1918 brought him sorrow beyond belief when he was informed about the death of his son, Algernon Parsons; he had been killed in action on April 26th 1918, in France. Algernon had been constantly in battle with the British Expeditionary Force in France from November 13th1914, until his death. His army career is just too vast and illustrious to list in a small work such as this, but his war was a long and hard one, he had been wounded on November 30th 1917, and many would be invalidated out, but Algernon's war wasn't yet over. He returned to battle only to die in action on the date stated. His body is buried at Lijssenthoek Military Cemetery in Belgium, Plot 28, and Row C. Grave 4.

Parsons' daughter Rachel was a Godsend to Charles over this period. She had been educated at Roedean and at Newnham. When at Cambridge she took mechanical science, and then she entered Heaton Works when her brother went to do his duty in France. She fully filled this role of directorship of the works. From 1922-1925 she served as a member of London County Council and she had the distinction of being one of the three woman members of the Institute of Naval Architects. Parsons was a sincere man, always having an air of refinement about him; he greeted friends warmly and with a smile. His handshake was curiously limp. Although he was a good conversationalist he was also a good listener too. Parsons loved the sea, being ever in the engine room or on the bridge. On cruisers, he visited Canada, South America and the West Indies.

In January 1931 he and Lady Parsons decided to travel to the West Indies on board the *'Duchess of Richmond'*, the voyage to Barbados was very enjoyable. Visits by him and Lady Parsons to Venezuela and Trinidad were interesting. They travelled by motor to Caracas and this did not agree with him, it was thought that coming straight from the English climate to tropical had caused his problem. Charles returned to the ship and spent the following day in his bunk thinking that he had a customary chill. There was apparently some problem with his circulation, but it was thought that it would improve with rest. Sadly, in Kingston Harbour on February 11th 1931, as the sun was setting, Charles Parsons slipped silently away.

The Realm of The Circling Sea

Admirals all, for Englands sake,
Admirals all, they said their say
(The echoes are ringing still),
Admirals All,they went their way,
To the haven under the hill.
But they left us a kingdom non-can take,
The realm of the circling sea,
To be ruled by the rightful sons of Blake
And the Rodney's yet to be

Honour is yours and fame!
honour as long as waves shall break
To Nelson's peerless name

(Henry Newbolt)

19

The 'Lusitania' & 'The Hood', the pride of the British Navy. 'Lusitania' sunk 7th. May 1915 and the 'Hood', 24th. May 1941. The tremendous loss of life was hard to bear by the British nation

Lusitania

HMS HOOD

The <u>Turbinia</u> at 33 knots; below <u>Charles Parsons</u> who dedicated his life to developing Turbine Engines that put England far ahead of any other Country in ships engines . Right on board the 'Turbinia which was his pride and joy:

WILLIAM COULSON
(& The Shaft Sinking Coulson's)

William Coulson was born at Gateshead Fell in 1791. He was undoubtedly one of the most eminent colliery sinkers in England. His sinking, up to the time of his death, was over a hundred pit shafts both in England and abroad, although a very high percentage of these were completed in the North of England.

In 1862 he led a heroic band of sinkers, when they tried to get 400-trapped miners out of the pit shaft at Hartley Colliery – where they were entombed. An engine beam had broken in the shaft and trapped the miners deep in the bowels of the pit. Coulson was in the area when he heard about the calamity at the pit, and he had no hesitation in going straight to the pit to try and get the men out. When he arrived at the pit everyone was at odds, and with his men he set to work with zeal and determination to clear the blockage in the shaft. Day after day they laboured, mostly without rest, and always the threat of gas and debris falling from above. Coulson and his men were not able to save any of the entombed men, but the sinkers never left their posts until all of the dead were out of that horrible pit. For their brave efforts William Coulson received a gold medal and his men were awarded silver medals from Queen Victoria.

William Coulson was a self-made man, beginning his life not unlike George Stephenson *(famous engineer)* as a trapper boy at a Northern pit. Coulson was not educated as such, learning what he could on his own account. He had an inborn genius for surmounting the highest obstacles of nature. His energy and industry made his name as a brilliant mining engineer of the times, and he had amazing perseverance.

Coulson had a family of four sons and three daughters. All of the family settled abroad, except for William, his son who accompanied him at Hartley Colliery. He carried on sinking collieries himself, and was also involved in a project putting a tunnel under the Mersey at Liverpool. He also founded Engineering Company at Crossgate Moor, Durham, where he lived. William Coulson (senior) in his early life, was employed at Walker Colliery, he worked a

20

full shift at the pit, then travelled to the Tyne where he worked a further shift as a trimmer at the docks. He showed amazing energy and industry. He came from a family of mainly Blacksmiths, his father grandfather and the Coulson descendants, worked for the Ravensworth Families for several generations. Coulson was involved in just about every colliery sank in the North of England over the forty years up to 1865. Even with the pits he did not sink, Coulson was usually consulted. The worst type of obstacles just was not a problem to him, with his practical knowledge and natural sagacity, they melted away and he quickly progressed the sinking.

His expertise and knowledge on sinking were even well known in countries abroad. For a number of years he developed mining resources in Prussia, mainly in the province of Westphalia. The work in these countries meant that he had to spend a great deal of time at sea, as well as on arduous trips in rough terrain overland. His gift for finding coal in the strata elevated him to high position amongst mining engineers of the day.

Besides his engagements in Prussia, the Austrian Empire had the benefit of his great experience in developing mining resources in that country. He was also engaged in ironstone mining in Prussia. Two of the best-known collieries that William Coulson sank in Prussia were the Hibernia and the Banrock. He also sank a great many pits in Wales when he gave a service to the Newport and Cardiff Ironstone Company. It was not only solving problems abroad that William Coulson was famous for, in this country there were many catastrophes which were linked to mining operations constantly happening when the North of England was trying to utilize its natural resources, and to keep people in employment. Mr. Coulson was the one who was always consulted.

In December 1856, William Coulson was invited to a complimentary dinner, by a number of Durham and Northumberland dignitaries. The dinner was held at the house of John Gowland, in Durham City. Mr. George Johnson, who was an intimate friend of Coulson's, occupied the chair. Through the chair he said he had known William Coulson for forty-five years. He was the first man ever to prove that coal existed below the magnesia limestone – these were the Collieries of Hetton in 1821. He proved this point, much to the delight and happiness of all concerned, including landowners, government and ordinary miners who relied on the industry for their living. It was from that time that he began to rise in the estimation of mining engineers and colliery viewers and owners – in fact *all* who were concerned in the development of Collieries. Coulson went from one difficult sinking, to another, non-proved beyond his reach, and that included the east coast collieries of Seaham, and other coastal pits. Most of these were plagued by water, tide, and also sand. He had an uncanny knack of producing coal in the strata; it was as if he could detect it with a dousing rod. Just about all of the pits that he sank produced coal in abundance.

The Coulson family was known in general for their sinking ability, in the North of England, the author's grandfather, great grandfather, and great great grandfather, were all Master Sinkers, and worked hand in hand with the great William Coulson. Indeed their ancestors like Coulson's, also worked as Blacksmith's for the Ravensworth Families. These were Joseph Coulson (born 1795), John Coulson (born 1820), and William Coulson (born 1860), *[named after the great man]*. All like William Coulson dedicated their lives to the North of England coalfield. In the 1851 census all can be seen together at Billy Row, with William Coulson, while sinking collieries like Roddymoor and others in the Crook and Southwest Durham area. William Coulson and his associates were credited with somewhere in the region of 100 shafts up to 1865. Some of the best known are as follows: Whitley, Walker, Seghill, Callerton, Harton, Hartley, Bedlington, North Seaton, Norwood, Crookhall, Roddymoor, Thickley, Pease's first Adelaide, Eldon, Blackboy (first pit), Whitworth, Bishop Middleham, Bowburn, Coxhoe, Crowtrees, West Hetton, Sherburn, Sherburn Hill, Philadelphia, Grange, Haswell, Thornley, Wingate, Castle Eden (two winning's), Seaton, Seaham, Framwelgate Moor, Waldridge Fell, Pelaw, and Urpeth. There were several sinking's in Lancashire, and North Wales also five collieries in Prussia. West Sleekburn, Bewick Main, Pease's Adelaide 1st & 2nd Collieries.

William Coulson commenced his career as a sinker at Thornley Colliery, where he worked sixteen-hour shifts. He even obtained material needed to commence the contract the following day; this was on top of the sixteen hours worked. William Coulson was much respected by his family and his men, they were very confident in his judgment. So much so that they would unhesitatingly enter very dangerous places in connection with the sinking operations.

In his private life he was a modest and a quiet man, who cared about people. He showed these attributes when risking his life to get the unfortunate men out of Hartley Colliery – he was seventy-one, at the time of the accident! He toiled relentlessly, with one thought in mind and that was to get these men back to their loved ones. When this was not achievable, there was no one more upset than Coulson. He toiled relentlessly on to get the dead out, so that their families could give them a Christian burial. Even with the constant threat of gas and falling debris, he and his men worked on, they did not relax until all of the men were at the surface.

William Coulson married twice; his second wife was Mary Hopper, who had a daughter Elizabeth, and son George, by her previous marriage. Both of these children were shown to be born at St. Helens, Auckland. William Coulson sank St. Helens Colliery. William Coulson married his second wife Mary Hopper

22

on 11th. November 1846. The certificate shows that at the time he lived at Shincliffe, just south of Durham City. William was ideally placed at the time to over see the many mining projects that was happening at this time and mainly on this route A177 to Stockton most of the Colliery shafts were put down. Some of these Collieries are Old Durham, Whitwell, Shincliffe, Coxhoe, Bowburn, Crowtrees, West Hetton, Bishop Middleham, Kelloe, Quarrington Hill, and Tursdale. I visited Shincliffe recently mainly to have a look at the area. I had not visited the village for some time. I realised just how well Coulson was positioned to the Collieries mentioned. There was also a road leading to old Sherburn and on to the coastal collieries. It seemed to me that Coulson also put a great deal of thought into living near to his projects. I also visited the parish church where he married Mary it was a beautiful church, set in a very picturesque village. The certificate also showed that John Coulson his father was also a miner and Mary Hopper's father was a shoemaker. His profession listed as 'Engine Man'. One other entry on his Marriage Certificate was that neither he nor his wife could read. But then neither could George Stephenson and many other well-known people that lived in that period. After completing his business in the south Durham area they travelled west to the area around Crook where the Pease's had mining interests. The whole family is shown on the 1851 census, living at 114 North Moor Cottages, Billy Row, and Crook. Joseph Coulson [author's G G Grandfather] lived at 110, North Moor Cottages, at the time, when sinking Roddymoor Colliery.

Untimely Death

On Monday 12th June 1865, William Coulson left his residence at Western Hill, Durham City, in his usual state of health. On this day he was due to attend a consultation at Hetton Hall, the residence of Nicholas Wood Esq. They were due to have a consultation with respect to a projected new sinking at Harton Colliery, near South Shields. The meeting had been due to take place at the Coal Trade Office, in Newcastle on Saturday.

Because of the absence of Mr. Collingwood, and L. Wood, this meeting had to be postponed until Monday at Mr. Wood's house. William Coulson arrived at the house on time and entered into consultation with Mr. Charles Alderson, from South Shields, together with Nicholas Wood, and Mr. Collingwood. The meeting progressed well until William Coulson felt ill with an attack of apoplexy – he was in much pain. Mr. Edgar, Surgeon, was called from Chester-Le-Street, and also Mr. S. Shiell, who came immediately. Mrs. Coulson and other members of his family were sent for and they quickly arrived, just before noon. Shortly after noon, Coulson had another attack, after which he was in much pain. From the commencement of the problem until the evening, William Coulson appeared to be in a great deal of physical pain, and the entire time unconscious. At 6.15

that evening, William Coulson, died leaving his family very distressed. His body was conveyed to Durham City arriving there at 1 am, Tuesday morning.

The funeral of William Coulson was held on Friday morning June 16th 1865, and it was exceptionally well attended with dignitaries, mining officials, mining engineers, coal owners, and many ordinary citizens who knew and respected him. His remains were buried at St. Margaret's Church Yard, Durham. One of the oldest Church's in Durham. The Church is very near to Crossgate where William Coulson and his family lived at that time.

After William Coulson died in 1865, the Authors family Coulson's continued this Amazing trade until coal mining was fully established in the north of England. Some Coulsons had broken away from the main family and established themselves in various areas of the North of England. Some of the family settled into other ways of making a living for their families; others were attracted to the early skills of their fore-fathers, in the art of sinking Colliery shafts into an abundance of coal for Colliery owners to make fortunes. Whenever there was any new sinking in the North of England a Coulson was not far away. The Author completed a 'Family History', on his particular family and traced his Grandparents and their parents before them, right into the present century finding every available census year, getting help in this task by following the sinkings at various areas of Durham. There were not two residences the same. The following is a brief progress of his particular side of the Coulson family on his mother's side, **Jane Fletcher Coulson**.

The Coulson's 1860-1909

The Author found them initially on the 1851 Census and already mentioned in the 'William Coulson' story. They were then found on the 1861 census at Stocks Row, Coxhoe. Great grandfather was based slightly towards Quarrington Hill, where an airshaft was being sunk at this exact time at Kelloe Colliery. William Coulson (Grandfather) was now part of the family aged [2]. My research shows that this particular Colliery was approx one mile from his present home, down a steep hill. The Census at Joint Stocks Row showed Ann Coulson *nee Robson*, living with her youngest son 'Robson', and named after her family. She was now [75], Joseph her husband had died at Grahamsley (Billy Row) where he was seen on the 1851 census with William Coulson, while sinking for the Pease's in the area especially at 'Roddy-Moor', this is where John Coulson (grandfather) and the Authors Great Grandfather had married Elspeth Wilson. The Census also showed that John's brother Joseph was also noticeable living a few doors away. The Author has old maps of the area, which shows Coxhoe Colliery which was part owned by Ann's brother *(Robson)*. The Map also shows Coxhoe Iron Works and also the Railway running directly through 'Stock's Row', where the Coulson's lived. It was obvious that the Coulson's were very

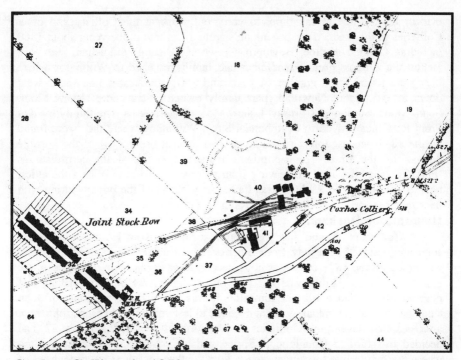

<u>Coxhoe Colliery in 1850</u>, shows the railway running directly through Joint Stock Row, to service Kelloe and complete the journey to Hartlepool; which was 14 miles distance. On route was a massive incline. The Coulson's were here mainly to sink the Colliery which was family owned by Robson & Jackson, & Ann's brother. John at this time was living a little further towards Kelloe; where records show, an air shaft was sunk at this exact time. There was also a series of bore holes put down; other pits were sank in the area such as Tursdale West Hetton, Bowburn and Crowtrees. This particular Coxhoe Colliery was worked out about 1857 and the family travelled again to the west of the County at Willington:

| Road, Street, &c. or No. or Name of House | HOUSES | | Name and Surname of each Person | Relation to Head of Family | Condition | Age of | | Rank, Profession, or Occupation | Where |
	In-habited	Unin-habited / Build-ing				Male	Female		
...ington Mill	1		John Coulson	Head	Mar	32		Coal Miner	Durham
			Elizabeth Do	Wife	Mar		23		Do
			William Do	Son		11		Scholar	Do
			Joseph Do	Son		6		Scholar	Do
	1		William Do	Son		2			Do
			Robert Pearson	Head	Mar	21		Back herman, Coal mine	Do
			Mary Do	Wife	Mar		22		Do
	1		Philip Robson	Head	Mar	39		Coal Miner	Do
			Margaret Do	Wife	Mar		31			Do

evident & in force at the time, to carry out work at the Colliery and other Collieries in the area. After the sinking's around Durham in the years about 1860 including Coxhoe, Kelloe, Bowburn, Crowtrees, Bishop Middleham and West Hetton the Authors great Grandfather and family travelled to Willington where they were based for a number of years and it was noticeable that shafts went down at Willington, Newfield (part family owned), Sunnyside, Ushaw Moor, South Moor, Burnhope, Cornsay, Ushaw Moor, Waterhouses. The family lived at Front Row then moved to Commercial Street Willington where they were found on the 1871 census. Johns wife Elspeth had died at Front Row of the horrible disease of the times 'Consumption', recorded on the death certificate as 'Phthisis', she was aged 36 leaving John to care for 5 boys. Wilson the eldest now 20, William, the Authors grandfather now 12 all of the boys working with their father at various Collieries in the area.

Holmside, nr. **Durham.**

Ten years on, and they were found at Sinkers Row, Holmside; Durham, John now married to a lady from Etherley, near Auckland Sarah Graham, who was noted on the 1871 census as housekeeper. It was noticeable that Wilson, the eldest boy in the family was not mentioned and it was obvious that he had married and started a life for himself. It was sad that the marriage of John Coulson and Sarah Graham was not destined to last very long, because John, now after years of developing Collieries in the North of England and now 52, had decided to return to Houghton le Spring and his roots, close to East Rainton where the family lived for many years; John's father Joseph at the time, head of the family. It was from here that they worked on the Earl of Durham's mining interests such as Pittington, Haswell, Elemore, Houghton and the Sherburn Collieries. It would seem that mainly due to his age John had decided to again settle in the area. John Coulson began work at South Hetton, the Colliery, where the Coulson's under William was credited with finding coal under the band of limestone in 1821. On 23rd. September 1881 John aged 53 & working as a Deputy and while drawing timber in a broken jud. died after being crushed under a heavy fall of stone, which came over the standing chocks.

On the 16th. April 1883 Grandfather William Coulson was married to Isabella Fletcher a woman with strong links to the hardy sea folk of Sunderland, her father Thomas Wiseman Fletcher was a Foreman Ship smith and her mother Jane Liddle, the daughter of a shipwright. The family were also heavily involved with rope making in the Sunderland dock areas. From Houghton-Le- Spring they travelled north of the county, William sinking pit shafts, like his father and ancestors before him. My mother Jane Fletcher Coulson was born at 'Westoe' South Shields on 6th. December 1893 where a second shaft for Westoe was sunk at this time 'St. Hilda's'.

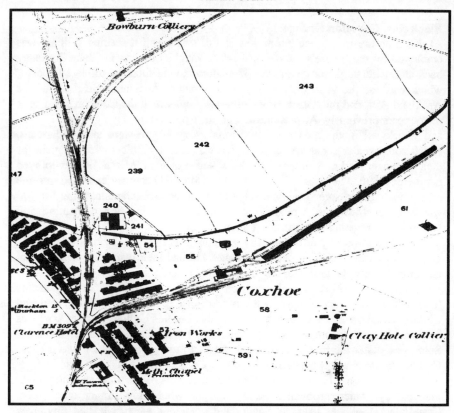

Above 1851 Coxhoe showing Coxhoe Iron works, Clayhole Colliery and Bowburn Colliery. The coal industry was thriving in the area at the time and so was the Clarence Railway, 'The Clarence Hotel shows in the drawing. Below the marriage of Grandfather William Coulson showing the sad death of his father John who had lost his life at South Hetton Colliery:

Black Boy, Coundon Grange.
At this time the Iron Stone boom was in full swing and it seemed William was employed by the 'Pease's', and Bolckow & Vaughan to sink for their Company back at Auckland, County Durham. The author found them on the latest census, which was for the year 1901 at Coundon Grange, Auckland. Nearby was the Auckland Park and the 'Black Boy Collieries', and which the Coulson's had sunk many years previously. At present the out-put from seams 'Five Quarter, Harvey and Brockwell in the area was 2000 tons a day. There were also 430 ovens, which converted the coal into coke, which was used by Bolckow & Vaughan for their own iron works. A firebrick works was also evident. Men & boys employed numbered 1600. The 'Black Boy', branch of the S&D railway extended into the area. Four villages sprang up & a school for mixed and infants catering for 700 was built in 1859 and a reading room was opened in 1868 containing 500 volumes, this together with the usual daily newspapers.

There were by now eight in the Coulson family and my mother had told me that they travelled from each pit village and had their own choir and musical instruments, my Grandfather & Grandmother were lay preachers, and they preached regular. Work was also carried out at 'Leasingthorne', colliery at this time, which was situated near to the present day road A689 to Rushyford and Chilton. Bolckow & Vaughan was also involved in this Colliery and the coal was in great demand to progress the production of Iron, Steel and other products. Some years later the family lived at 44 West Chilton Terrace, which was a Pease Colliery house. Later when Pease's Chilton Colliery was sunk, my grandparents were situated here. I have covered Newspaper reports of the time, and the pit was plagued by water problems. Sadly this is where my grandmother died, Grandfather took her back to Sunderland cemetery where she had obviously requested to be interred, and where they had a double grave. My mother spoke at length of her tremendous loss when her mother died so young, she always said that she was 40 but infact she was 43 when she passed away. My mother was 15 on this unhappy occasion an age when a mother's attention was important.

On the 6th January 1903 John Coulson's eldest son Wilson was killed at Willington Colliery aged [52]. Some years later there had been a spate of explosions in the East Durham area in the early years of the 19th Century and on the 16th February 1909, Stanley Colliery exploded. William Coulson having helped to sink the Colliery some years previously and knowing the pit well, offered his services, many other experienced mining engineers did the same. William Coulson had to get hold of the centre cage rope to save him from falling into the shaft. This later caused blood poisoning in his legs. Surgery was necessary to combat the poison and it was from his deathbed he wrote a monologue '*The West Stanley Disaster*', he finally died 15th. April 1917.

Because of the development of mining in the north of England and because of the involvement of the Coulson family it was inevitable that there would be causalities among them. There was in fact 26 members of the family killed from 1778 which included John, our great grandfather and his first born son Wilson who was killed at Willington Colliery, County Durham, in 1903. The Following is a list of these brave men.

The Coulson Family Death's in Durham Collieries
1778-1948

Benjamin W. Coulson	35	13 Nov. 1925	Browney	Dur.
Christopher Coulson	11	16 Sept. 1873	Houghton	Dur
E.G. Coulson	30	15 Dec. 1942	Houghton	Dur.
Edward Coulson		1917	Bebside	NBL.
Frederick Coulson	19	29 March 1911	Roanhead	Lan.
George Coulson	14	27Nov. 1891	Murton	Dur.
J. Coulson	67	14 Apr. 1948	Craghead	Dur.
John Coulson (jun)	20	11 Dec.1877	South Tyne	Nbl.
John Coulson	33	16 Jan. 1862	New Hartley	NBL
John Coulson	55	29 Jan. 1869	Springwell	Dur.
John Coulson (G/Grand Father.)	53	23Sept.1881	South Hetton	Dur.
Joseph R. Coulson	19	11Jan. 1887	Littleburn	Dur.
Joseph William Coulson		1935	Montagu	NBL
Matthew Coulson	20	16 Feb. 1909	West Stanley	Dur.
Patrick Coulson	28	03 Nov. 1887	Hamsteels	Dur.
Robert Coulson	26	16Jan. 1862	New Hartley	NBL
Thomas Coulson		08Dec. 1778	Dolly Pit Chaytors	H.Dur.
Thomas Coulson	13	24Nov. 1879	Urpeth	Dur.
Thomas Coulson	27	10 Nov.1883	South Durham	Dur.
Thomas Coulson	15	24 Apr.1891	Murton	Dur.
Thomas Coulson	62	16 Feb. 1909	West Stanley	Dur.
Thomas J. Coulson		19 Apr. 1882	West Stanley	Dur.
Thomas J. Coulson		1929	North Walbottle	NBL.
William Coulson	15	24 Nov. 1872	Wearmouth	Dur.
William G. Coulson		1940 Backworth	Fenwick Pit	NBL.
Wilson Coulson(G/Grandfathers first Son)	52	6 Jan.1903	Willington	Dur.

__William Coulson__ and his men at Hartley pit top, this is the disaster that made Queen Victoria weep:

Hetton Colliery, where **William Coulson** *proved that coal existed below the Magnesium limestone; Hetton was also where Stephenson tested his Locomotion 1*

HETTON COLLIERY.

Hartley Colliery, where William Coulson failed to get over 400 entombed miners out of the one shaft mine

The Hartley Medals awarded to the brave sinkers Coulsons was gold the others silver; designed by Mr. Wyon of the mint

1851 Census at Billy Row, *the census shows the Authors Great Grandfather Joseph Coulson 66 with his wife Ann Robson. The Census also shows* **William Coulson** *living at 114 with his second wife Mary Hopper, Hartley Disaster had not yet happened. The Census also shows Joseph's oldest son living two doors away. They were all busy sinking pits for the Pease's interests Roddymoor was sunk at this time:*

JOHN HARRISON
(Accurate maritime clock maker)

John Harrison was born at Foulby Village, Pontefract, Yorkshire, in 1693. The exact date is unknown. It is a fact that Harrison was dead before the rise of the Great Engineers of the 18th. Century, which revolutionized our country, but he contributed as much as any of them.

Harrison was a mechanical genius; he contributed so much to the evolution of our society, which these days are regulated by high speeds and technology. John Harrison produced an. accurate means of telling the correct time with a mechanical clock. It is debatable that anyone has ever made *anything* mechanical more accurate, even in this modern society. As technology improved up with modern means of shipping, transport overland, and flight, this could not be achieved without positive and completely accurate timekeeping. One second out in calculating a course by sea land or air would lead to being miles off course.

John Harrison had a very humble beginning; his parents were simply unimportant people. His father, Henry Harrison, was a carpenter and worked for a local landowner, Sir Roland Winn, who lived at Nostel Priory. The reason why John's exact birthday was not known was probably because of their humble beginnings, and nobody much cared that his birth had not been registered in the parish register. Education as early as the 17th century was rare for commoner's children and John only learned the basics, of reading and writing. Because of this he was never able to express himself throughout his life, and explanations of his ideas were always a problem. What *is* known however is that John Harrison was fascinated by any machinery with wheels or cogs, which included windmills and waterwheels – they simply amazed him. Clocks in such a small village, as Foulby, except possibly at his father's employer's house, were extremely rare. In fact it was at Nostel Priory (fathers employer) where he first saw a clock, and he gazed at it in amazement. The slowly swinging pendulum fascinated him and he listened to the striking of the hours and half hours. Then his gaze shifted to the movement of the toothed wheels inside of the case. The whole movement of this clock fascinated him, so much so that he could watch it all day. When John Harrison was seven years of age, the family moved from Foulby to Barrow-

28

upon-Humber where his father's employer had another estate. This was a distance of some 50 miles and the journey had to be covered by walking, carrying what few goods they had, with a packhorse loaned from their father's employer. Most village children of this age never ever ventured far away from their village, and now John was travelling fifty miles! He was very excited about the journey. Early one morning the family set out to travel to their new home at Barrow. The tracks were rough and deeply rooted and for most of the year extremely muddy. The family, after a hard and weary journey, eventually reached Barrow, their new home. John found his new village far more interesting than the old village of Foulby and a short distance from it was the river Humber.

The port of Kingston-on-Hull stood on the opposite bank. John and James his brother spent many hours watching the coming and going of large ships into and out of the port, little did John realize at this point just how important his invention would be to the navigation of these same ships that he was watching. The local village Parson befriended John and developed his reading and writing ability. He only possessed one book on Philosophy, by a priest called Nicholas Sanders, who died in 1581. The subject of Philosophy did not interest John one bit but it was a book nevertheless, and a basis for furthering his reading and writing skills. John copied down every word in the book together with every diagram. He did this over and over again until he could memorize the words. He kept copies of this throughout his life, as evidence of his reading and writing capabilities.

John Harrison eventually became a carpenter, following his father into this trade. He also made money surveying and measuring land and this shows that the vicar even tutored him in maths. He certainly knew how to calculate, as the timepieces that he made at this time would not be accurate. His father taught him the arts of producing artistic things out of wood and he used carpenter's tools to perfection. Over the last few years he had noticed and studied the movement of clocks in other people's homes, and he had memorized these. He would soon produce a clock of his own design out of wood using the techniques his father had taught him.

One of the obvious problems that Harrison was coming up against was friction. Light lubricants were just not available in 1715, resulting in even a small amount of friction upsetting the fine and delicate mechanism. Harrison worked out that wood rather than metal would be prone to less friction, and he was also aware that some woods were naturally self-lubricated. The amount of work needed to construct the clock was astronomical. Each of the toothed wheels were made in 4 segments and these were put together by two circular layers of wood, one on each side, which were smaller in size so they did not overlap the teeth. Oak was used because of its hardness and one can imagine the extreme accuracy needed to cut the teeth on the circumference of each wheel. They had to exactly correspond. The face of the clock was made out of metal, and the figures and the divisions were scribed very finely on its service. John and his brother, James, made a number of these long case clocks, which had wooden wheels. There are a number of these clocks still in the museum of the Clockmakers Company in London.

John Harrison certainly wasn't going to be satisfied with his first clock. He knew that although his initial clock was good, there were many improvements that could be made. His inspiration was in producing a clock with accurate time. What he had to consider was temperature changes. A good timekeeper in winter would lose in summertime. The metal on the pendulum expanding in the heat and contracting in cold weather brought this on. The longer a pendulum is, the slower it swings and though the difference in length is slight the inaccuracy in time is considerable.

It took an ingenious person like Harrison to realize a way round the problem. There are no two metals that expand equally with heat. Harrison carefully picked out steel and brass. Brass expands nearly half as much again as steel in heat. Harrison made his pendulum in the form of a gridiron, with alternate rods of brass and steel. Each pair being firmly joined at one of three to two. When assembled, the downward expansion of steel exactly compensates the upward expansion of brass rods and thus the pendulum remained at a constant length. Gridiron pendulums may still be seen on older clocks. John discovered other problem solvers, one known as *'grasshopper escapement'*, this shifts the power from the slowly falling weights to the pendulum and the other called the 'going ratchet' this enables the clock top, to keep going when being wound. This is important, because of the period spent winding the clock and would be fully explained in a book of 'Horology'.

The real challenge came to Harrison in 1713 when the government offered and indeed passed an act offering a reward of £10,000 and £20,000 to anyone who could find an accurate method of calculating 'Longitude', on board ships at sea, to within 60-40 or even 30 miles. In those days this money was a massive amount, and the government did not offer this without good reason. The government felt that 'Longitude', was important enough to offer this money. When shipping, or aircraft is in distress, Longitude and Latitude, for the precise position is needed, Latitude is given in degrees, minutes and seconds north or south. Longitude is given in the same measurement east and west. If these can be given a rescue can be started. The formula for calculating this came when navigators discovered that at the Equator the sun is directly overhead at noon, so it became a matter of measuring the angle of the sun with the horizon at the same hour to discover how far to the north or the south of the equator the observer was.

The matter of determining Longitude at sea was at one time not even considered, until ships travelled long distances. Prior to the 16th Century, ships just did not venture far at all, possibly a few hundred miles from shore. When they began to get more adventurous and sailed over this limit, to say, over a thousand miles across the Atlantic, *then* Longitude became very important.

Ships were being lost; sailors were losing their lives as land approached before they had estimated – especially at night. The king of Spain was thought to be the first to offer a large reward for calculating Longitude. When people first pondered the question of Longitude, they found that it was closely related to time. Noon in London is midnight half way around the world, half way between these two points to the west of London, say 'Chicago', America, it will be 6am. But to the east, in say Siberia, it will be 6pm. If 24 equidistant lines were drawn from the north to south poles, the time by the sun would vary by exactly one hour from line to line. Twenty-four lines would be too few for accuracy, so the world was divided up to 360 lines of longitude, each being I degree from the next. The imaginary line running from pole to pole and passing through Greenwich was fixed as the line of 0 degrees longitude, because an observatory was established there in 1675, and the first Astronomer Royal was John Flamstead, who happened to be one of the pioneers in the search for the calculation of Longitude.

The imaginary line through Greenwich is still used throughout the world, as the point from which all Longitude is reckoned, and expressed as so many degrees east or west of Greenwich. In the same way Greenwich time became the time from which all time in the world was set. An example of longitude and time is as follows: The master of a vessel, which has steamed due west in the Atlantic, observes the sun when it is due north, which means that at that time it is precisely noon. He has in his possession a very accurate clock, which has been set at Greenwich time on the day that the ship sailed. He checked the clock and found that it read 3 pm, showing that at this spot at sea; there is a difference of 3 hours between sun time and Greenwich time. One hour represents 15 degrees, which means that the ship is 45 degrees west of Greenwich, and somewhere to the North East of Newfoundland. A very accurate timepiece can calculate this Longitude. The act of Parliament of 1713 did not mention this fact and offered prize money merely for the discovery of a method of finding Longitude at sea, within 60,40, or 30 miles. Many suggestions were put forward, some strange, others quite odd, but still after 15 years the prizes were not won. It was not easy in those days, even to hear of any acts passed by Government, especially living in obscurity as Harrison was. Somehow, however, John did find out, possibly from another clockmaker, and he decided to take up the challenge.

The Government set up a special body called, 'the Board of Longitude', to deal with the flood of ideas submitted. The year was 1728 and John Harrison

31

set off early one morning to travel to London, with a drawing of an instrument carefully rolled for carrying purposes, which he thought may be successful in calculating Longitude. His idea he thought was spot on, but he required from the government body the finance to produce the instrument, which he had in mind and which he knew in his heart would succeed. To build it would cost a great deal of money. This showed that in 1728 John Harrison was still a relatively poor man, without education to set his idea in writing. Lack of money humbles the best of men and Harrison showed terrific strength of character on that morning when he set out, but he was driven on, by his absolute confidence in his idea. It was thought that Harrison walked the full distance to London from Barrow on Humber, carrying his precious life's work with him.

Eventually Harrison arrived at London, where he was extremely fortunate to meet up with Edward Halley, who at the time was 'Astronomer Royal'. Harrison showed him his drawings. At this time Halley was over 70 years old and he was on the Board of Longitude. Knowing fully well, that no advance would be forthcoming from the Board of Longitude, Halley advised John to go to see a person called George Graham. Graham was reputed to be the finest clockmaker in London, and successor to the great Thomas Tampion, he was also a very kind man. Graham was a Quaker and believed it was wrong to charge or receive interest on money. All of his cash, he kept in a strong box as he did not believe in banks. George Graham liked John Harrison, so much so, that he gave him an interest free loan of £200 and told him to go back to Barrow and make his clock, and re-approach them when it was complete.

John Harrison took Graham's advice, and anyway he wished to see his family again, this was the first time away from home and he missed them terribly. Harrison's clock was not completed for 7 years. When seeing the clock at the Maritime Museum at Greenwich it's not hard to see why it took the time it did, not forgetting that as well as making the clock John had to also make a living. The timepiece is very large weighing 70 pounds. The movement is very delicate and has an intricate mechanism, the explanation of which would be beyond the scope of this book. It is a clock, but a clock built to withstand the rolling and pitching of a ship in rough sea, and still keep the correct time. It is not hard to see that John Harrison was a genius; it was completely made out of metal to the finest limits. Each part being hand made, and not accepted by Harrison until it actually was perfect, even if he had to start the part all over again.

John Harrison was capable of exquisitely accurate workmanship and it showed in the end product. Later, when Harrison produced other clocks for sea going ships, it was easy to see that he had not only built them to withstand rough sea and to keep exact time, but he also built them to gaze at, and marvel at his engineering skills and exquisite workmanship – it showed pure devotion to the trade of a clockmaker.

John Harrison completed to his own satisfaction his timepiece to calculate Longitude. The problem now was to transport it to London, from Barrow-on-Humber. Roads were virtually non-existent as early as 1700. Muddy dirt tracks with deep-rooted terrain were very evident. There was, however, a stage coach that only ran in the summer months, they covered 20 or 30 miles a day at the most, and would take six or seven days to reach London. He would have to completely dismantle his clock; this he did reassembling it on arrival in the capital. Actually, the journey was a nightmare for him. These were the days of the highwaymen and John had 7 years of hard work packed in a crate. The chances were that he would not have much sleep at all, until his arrival at London; but somehow, through sheer determination, they arrived safely.

Edward Halley was the first to see the clock working and he was very impressed and amazed at the quality of workmanship combined with such an accurate timepiece. Halley was still Astronomer Royal. The second man to see the clock was George Graham, his benefactor. Both Halley and Graham gave Harrison certificates of approval and ordered that the clock should be submitted to the board of Longitude. The board, unable to differ from the other eminent members, also accepted and ordered it to be tested at sea. As it happened the board took their time in this matter and it took a year before it was put on board a vessel. This was H.M.S. Centurion; together with John they sailed for Lisbon in 1736. This ship was a man-of-war and the crew and everyone else connected to the test treated John with great respect. They were about to solve the problem of Longitude.

On reflection, it seemed a little waste of time this venture, as the whole voyage was in a North South direction. Still, the Bay of Biscay would thoroughly test the clock in rough seas. Even with the facts of the present voyage John was able to correct a navigational problem of over one degree, if they had been going a greater distance they would have been many miles off course. A full report was given and the Board offered Harrison £500, they would pay half now with the other half after the completion of a further clock, more accurate, even though the first was well within the limit requested.

Graham was not very happy at all about the situation, thinking that the full prize should have been paid or, failing that, at least £1000, but the Board wanted their value, and John received only £250. John Harrison decided he would accept the Board's offer, even though he was unhappy. This was a further challenge, and anyway, he fully intended bettering his timepiece even though his first was accurate to the Board standards. He set about making a further Marine Chronometer, and for this purpose came to live in London, and he set about

33

devoting his whole life to the project. It took John Harrison three years to complete his work, and it was generally thought that he made it in his spare time, as the money given to him by the Board of Longitude was hardly enough to make the clock without having to live, and he would have to work to feed himself. It was generally thought that work would not be a problem for John as a person clever as he was with watch making, could easily get work. There was still also the loan to Graham outstanding.

It was 1739 when the second watch was completed it was smaller than his first and easier to handle. The board as promised, paid him the promised £250, then a further £500 for another Chronometer. Harrison had already started on this even before he received the second amount. It seemed that he felt inside that he could always do better and he *did* do better. John Harrison promised the board that indeed it would be better than the other two. The Longitude Board must have wondered about this statement as it took John Harrison 17 years to complete. This timepiece was much smaller than the others and it was extremely accurate, the margin of error being 4 seconds a week. This time he was awarded a gold medal for the excellence of his timepiece; he still knew in his heart that he could still do better so consequently, he started on a new timepiece.

John Harrison's fourth Chronometer was a surprising change from his normal clocks. It was not much larger than a normal pocket watch. It was about five inches in diameter and it only took Harrison two years to complete. The experts of the time thought that this timepiece was just about as perfect as you could get a watch to be. In his book 'The Marine Chronometer', R.T. Gould said that for beauty and accuracy and also historical interest, *"it must take pride of place as the most famous Chronometer that was ever made, or for that matter ever will be made".*

All of John Harrison's clocks can be seen at the National Maritime Museum at Greenwich, there are also large photographs at the science Museum. John Harrison was 66 years of age when he completed this particular timepiece in 1759. Did he win the prize offered by the Board of Longitude? No! He had been inspired all of his life by this prize, he had bettered his timepiece each time to well within the standards required but they still did not pay him. He had received nothing like the money offered. He had conquered Longitude; by making a near perfect as possible timepiece, he was a very disappointed and disillusioned man.

Graham and Halley were a long time dead at this time in Harrison's career, so no backing from within was forthcoming when Harrison completed his fourth timepiece. This Chronometer was 5 1/2 inches in diameter driven by a steel spring. It had a fitted device with two metals to combat expansion as was earlier invented by John. This corrected any variation there may be because of heat. Harrison was extremely confident that it would stand up to any test, and subsequently he asked the board to give it the stringent of tests at sea and they agreed.

A voyage to the West Indies was arranged, John Harrison was by then too old to go to sea on the voyage, his son William went instead. The voyage was arranged for the 18th November 1761, on the ship '*H.M.S. Deptford*'. William was on board with his father's precious Chronometer. They arrived back in England four months later; the timepiece lived up to expectations losing only five seconds on arrival at Jamaica. Over the whole trip, including the return journey, it was within 2 minutes thus qualifying easily for the top prize of £20,000, but the Board of Longitude still refused to pay. The excuses for this was simply amazing saying [1] it could be a fluke, and another trial should be carried out, [2] he should divulge how the timepieces were made. John Harrison was born in Yorkshire and having all of the characteristics of a Yorkshire man, refused these demands. Even though he was now old and thoroughly fed up with the Board's sharp practice, he petitioned Parliament, resulting in the Board of Longitude having to pay him £5000 immediately and they had also to give him back his timepieces. Justice, in part, was seen to be done.

John Harrison

Harrisons first clock

*Top left, **Harrisons** second clock 1737; right the third clock 1759; lower left and right , on the left produced like a pocket watch. **Captain Cook** took an exact copy[5] on his voyage and it was so accurate he was convinced it was a fluke:*

John Harrison was now over 70 but his eyes and hands were still perfect. He sent his Chronometer to the Greenwich Observatory for testing. He then sent it on a second voyage to the West Indies and Barbados. Again, William went representing his father on the voyage. After 7 weeks voyage the results were just as spectacular as the other voyages. The error was only half a minute fast. Back in Portsmouth after five months it was still less than one minute out. This was no less than excellent. But they still haggled, and they still were not satisfied, and would not pay the prize. John Harrison again petitioned Parliament, then even King George III. He appealed successfully and in 1772 when Harrison was 79 he received the full award.

John Harrison lived until he was 83, so his final years at least were spent in relative comfort. The Science Museum, in South Kensington, London holds Harrison's Grandfather Clock dated 1715, on the dial is inscribed 'J. N. Harrison', Barrow. The clock is completely constructed of wood except the escape wheel. This is Harrison's first clock, and after 300 years it would still work perfectly and includes the day of the month. John Harrison was a credit to his profession and many early seamen would be thankful that he conquered the calculation of Longitude with his engineering techniques and his amazing clock.

SIR ALLIOTT VERDON ROE
(first British powered flight)

During the war, Belfast Airport was an RAF Coastal Command Station. From here regular patrols into the Atlantic were made. Sometimes the patrols did escort work; other times they did anti-submarine work. A reliable plane was needed for these patrols – this was mainly low flying, as there tended to be very low cloud. It was not unusual for planes to just disappear as low cloud quickly dropped and the Atlantic was so vast. Early planes were not very satisfactory, and aircrews lost their confidence in the aircraft. Suddenly, new aircraft appeared at the station, and these were very suitable for the job in hand. The prototype of these aircraft first flew in 1935 and were powered by two 350 hp. Engines having a range of 800 miles, top speed of 188 mph at 7000 feet, cruising speed of 158 mph, at 6000 feet and a ceiling of 19,000 feet. It carried a crew of three, being easy to fly and completely reliable. This plane renewed the confidence in the station. The aircraft was the Avro Anson. It served the RAF in this area for the rest of the war and a long time after.

The Lancaster and Shackleton, then later the Vulcan (V. Bomber), all came from Avro, all of these played their own part for the RAF, especially the Lancaster which was a brilliant bomber. One of the original engineers of this amazing company survived being swallowed up later by Avro Anson, he was Sir Alliott Verdon Roe. He was born in Manchester out of a family of seven and his father was a doctor. Verdon attended St. Paul's school, where it was found that he excelled in athletics. He wasn't so bright at school and he left as soon as possible to help his father earn money to help keep the rest of the family. His father did not push the possibility of extra education when he did leave school as he thought that Verdon was an under-achiever. He did however allow him to go to British Columbia to learn Civil Engineering.

After a period helping to survey for a railway, which was still in its early stages, he returned to start a five-year apprenticeship at the old Lancashire &

Yorkshire railway. After finishing his time he worked as a fitter at Portsmouth Dockyard, and he also studied for a while at Kings College, London. He sat an engineering examination for the Royal Navy as an Engineer, passing the engineering part but failing badly in mathematics. He went to sea as an engineer working for the African Royal Mail Company. It was at this time he became interested in flight.

One day he watched the elegant flight of an albatross off the coast of Africa. The bird actually keeping up with the ship, without any effort. He felt sure this was down to the shape of the bird, and in his spare time made models of planes as near as possible to the Albatross. He then launched them from the side of the ship, expecting them to take flight and glide like the Albatross. The rest of the crew was rather amused. Initially the model just did nothing and fell into the sea, but the more he got his model shaped like the bird he had been observing, it started to take flight and glide, staying in the sky for a long time even rising with the under currents. This inspired Roe and when the ship docked he decided to quit his ship and look further into powered flight.

Doctor Roe was not very impressed by his son's decision but he was assured that he would work to keep himself, with a job in the Motor Industry. Verdon read all he could with regard to flight, and then he decided to write to Wilbur Wright, the American who was the first man ever to fly a powered Aeroplane. In 1906 he wrote a letter to the Times saying that although Wright had flown twenty miles, in America, no one seemed interested at all in England, he further remarked in his letter that if steps were taken in this country there is no reason why a powered flight cannot take place in this country, by the summer. The engineering editor replied that any attempt at flight was doomed to failure and very dangerous to human life. An advertisement appeared in the media for a secretary for The Aero Club (mainly ballooning). Roe applied for the position, and although not having the qualifications as such, he got the job; the reasoning being in Roe's reckoning was that he might meet others with similar interests in powered flight. Roe's first introduction to powered flight was by way of a model, a London Newspaper had advertised a competition with a prize of £150, for anyone who could build a model of not less than two pounds and fly it by propelled flight at least one hundred feet. Roe built three models in his brother's stables at Putney, the largest having a wingspan of eight feet and weighing five pounds. He propelled the machine by means of twisted elastic.

This competition was held at Alexander Palace and Roe won a total of £250 according to the classification, but he wasn't going to get cash that easily and he only received £75 from the organizers who said that the entries did not justify all of the prize money. Verdon Roe was disappointed but didn't show it, he knuckled down and used the small amount to build an aeroplane. Roe's first plane was a monstrosity with no fuselage or tail. The elevator was in front of the propeller, behind the biplane wings. The pilot, or aviator, sat in the front of the engine. The whole thing ran on four wheels and the plane was built at his brother's premises, where he had his daily surgery (his brother now a Doctor).

Roe's plane was called Roe it was 23 feet long, the wingspan being thirty feet – all powered by a 9-hp. Motorcycle engine. His plane was completed in September 1907, when he decided to compete for a prize of £2500 offered for a first powered flight of a full size aeroplane. The competition was to be held at Brooklands motorcycle track at Weybridge. One condition was that the flight had to take place by the end of the year. A covered building had to be built to house the plane, and when he had completed it he found that the engine wasn't big enough to lift the machine off the ground. Some kind person lent him a 2Ohp French Antoinette engine, which he accepted, but alas the engine arrived too late for the competition, and his chance was lost. Roe did however try his plane out. He drove it round and round the track. A car towed him with rope. The wheels having no springs were jumping and juddering on the field, and then he was momentarily airborne. This happened a number of times and each time Roe was able to land. Roe devised a system to let go of the tow rope after which the plane glided to a halt, most times crashing, and sometimes putting Roe in danger. Most times he had to repair his plane. The Brookland track manager ordered Roe off the track and he found he had nowhere to go. He finally found a field elsewhere, on part of a swampland, and he spent the very last of his money on posts for his shed.

Verdon Roe was just about destitute, he had to live in the shed and he had just five shillings a week to feed himself. The manager of the field forbade him to sleep on the premises and Verdon left the shed to return later to sleep in a packing case. It was about this time that he managed to fit his Antoinette engine but found it too powerful for his prop, which snapped at full power, and he later strengthened it.

The date was June 1908, Verdon brought out his machine as normal early one morning, as he was permitted to try the machine only early in the morning. He checked out everything, and then started his machine and brought it to full power. Roe used the elevator and the front wheels came off the ground. The plane was completely on its back wheels, then without warning, it was airborne, the plane was in flight. This was the moment that Verdon had been dreaming of ever since observing the albatross in flight off the African coast. Verdon Roe gently eased his machine down. The plane had flown a hundred yards and there had been none to observe it. The truth of the matter was, Roe had been the first British plane to fly. After this great breakthrough, the manager of Brooklands track caused Roe much distress by first of all hiring his plane shed at ten shillings a day the condition was that Roe had to remove his machine first, and make sure it was out of sight. Roe took his plane away from its shed and it resulted in some men carrying it away dropping it down a depression where it was found to be beyond repair. Roe had still not experienced the worst, he was now told to remove his shed within two days, or sell it to the manager for £15 – it having cost him £60 in the first place.

Roe had no alternative but let his shed go and he was now exactly back where he had started, he returned his engine to France and all he had left in the world was his 9 hp engine. Roe was not beaten, he returned to Putney where he built a plane around his engine. This one was rather different, it had a fuselage, and tail, the prop and engine were at the front. He actually made his plane a tri-plane with three planes in the tail also. The framework was made of wood, including the wings, held tight with piano wire and covered with muslin backed cotton oiled paper, for which he had paid two pence a yard. The under carriage was two bicycle wheels on forks and also a bicycle wheel at the back. To act as a shocker for himself and the petrol tank he used elastic straps.

Roe called his plane *'Bulls Eye, Avro Plane'*, with Roe on board it still only weighed 400 pounds. There was a worry whether the 9hp engine would ever be able to lift the plane off the ground. Roe decided to test the plane at Lea Marshes north east of London, where there was about half a mile square open ground, if rather muddy. The River Lea was on one side and a railway line on the other. Two unused railway arches adorned the field in which Roe kept his machine and where he also lived. For cooking and keeping warm Roe used an iron brazier. The only time he ever left his machine was to go to France where Wilber Wright was giving exhibitions of flight near Paris. Roe cycled to Southampton taking his bicycle on the boat then he rode a hundred miles to St Malo where the exhibition was being held.

Wilbur Wright and Verdon Roe over this period had a long talk, and Roe was allowed to inspect his plane. Soon he had to return to England where he again cycled all the way he had come the following day and he was quickly back with his machine. The date was 1909; Roe was now ready for a trial flight. 'Bulls Eye' at first only covered about twenty yards at a height of two yards, the plane then tipped over to one side on its wing hitting the ground. Roe fixed the damage then tried again and the same thing happened. He soon found it was caused by a gusty wind, and he soon learnt to control the plane. With practice, he was soon flying a hundred yards at a height of ten feet. These flights were monitored and later accepted as being the first ever-British flights by British Aircraft and British Pilot, over British land and this success spurred Roe on.

The overall opinion at the time with the public and the media was that he was a crank and madman. In July 1909 something happened to change this, and make people think differently. M. Lois Bleriot, the French Aviator, landed in Dover after flying over the Channel. From that moment people started to sit up and take interest. All of a sudden displays were arranged; at Blackpool in particular £150 was offered to anyone who could fly a plane over a hundred yards, this was open to any British citizen. On paper seemed easy for Roe but again fate was to intervene. Roe took his machine to Blackpool and the very day of the show it rained as if it had never rained before. The oilpaper covering most of the plane got soaked, and it could only manage fifty yards. This was at the expense of taking the plane there and back just for nothing.

There was further harassment back at the field when the Local Council considered his trials were a nuisance and barred him from flying when cattle were in the vicinity, grazing, they also barred him otherwise as being a nuisance. Roe just could not win he was being harassed by narrow-minded people in power. He moved on to Wembley Park. Roe by now was an expert at the controls of his machine and indeed had to be, as this place was used for sport. Roe had crashes, one in particular was on the cricket pitch and he was pleasantly surprised when the players actually helped him, even removing any hindrance to his flying efforts such as boarding, etc. By this time Roe's cash situation was desperate he owed his father £300 and his brother £150. Although there was no family pressure, at all, indeed they carried on backing him especially seeing his enthusiasm. Eventually Roe managed to build, with his brother's help, at Manchester, a small aeroplane factory, and managed to sell a tri-plane. He then found the perfect place to practice flying, this was back at Brooklands, a new Manager had taken over and he was very interested in flight, he also constructed a strip for taking off and landing within Brooklands. To cap it all he even supplied hangers! Things seemed to happen all of a sudden for Verdon Roe, and he pushed on, again with his brother's financial help, to build a further bi-plane.

Realizing that the 9 hp. Engine was not suitable, he bought two 35hp engines fitting them on to two more planes. Initially there were problems but eventually, after adjustments, the machine took off and climbed steadily, but when trying to level off, Roe found that he had a problem. The only way round this he thought was cutting the engine speed and allowing the plane to stall and drop to the ground. Roe injured himself and the plane was in a bit of a mess. Roe thought deeply about the problem and decided that the weight was too far back. He adjusted the tail accordingly and Roe IV worked perfectly.

Competitions seemed to be bad luck for Roe. There was a further competition in 1910 at Blackpool and again Roe entered, this time leaving nothing to chance he entered two machines. The planes being dismantled and sent by train. The packing boxes were in the carriage next to the engine, and they were covered with tarpaulin. Both planes were destroyed completely, the rail

41

Company denying responsibility as the planes travelled at the owner's risk. It was a complete loss to Roe; the planes were worth £1500. He would still not be beaten and within four days built another at his Manchester factory, ordering an engine from the makers to be delivered straight to Blackpool. Roe spent all night assembling the engine. The plane was ready two hours before the show and he had time for one short test flight. His troubles were still not over and both his tyres burst, leaving him just rims to take off with. The plane played up, as it had not been tested properly and he narrowly missed crashing into the crowd, but his skill prevented this. For all of his efforts Roe was awarded a consolation prize of £75. It was about this time that he travelled to America to demonstrate the aeroplane he had sold there to Harvard University. Up to that point it had never flown. Roe also took with him the machine that had got him out of trouble at Blackpool. As it happened, in America he had trouble with both machines, he actually fell over sixty feet after a stall. This was reputed to have been the worst accident in his life. Roe was rushed to Hospital with blood flowing from a head wound. After three days he was out again busy with his machine. One plane was produced from the two he had taken to America and Harvard bought this one.

Roe built one more tri-plane, and then he reverted back to two wings in 1909. This was a 50hp Gnome engine, with a top speed of 65mph. It was an exceptionally safe machine and later many pilots preferred it to learn to fly in. This was the first Avro School. It was first decided in 1911 that the Avro should not be a warplane but the War department decided to have a competition, to find a machine with their specifications. They did this having a warplane with a specific specification in mind. Nine months were allowed to build the machine. It was to be crewed by two people, and should be able to stay in flight four and a half hours with a full load. Speed in still air should 55 mph, and it would have a rate of climb of 200 feet per minute for a thousand feet. It would also have to maintain a height of 4500 feet for one hour. The plane must arrive in packing cases by railway, and be easily assembled.

This was open to the whole world, prizes being 1. £4000, 2. £2000. A class was also reserved for British designers with a first prize of £1500. This was thought a snub to early aeroplane pioneers. The War Office further said that they would not buy any British made machines, as they felt there were none safe enough; they said however that they were prepared to buy a French plane. A.V. Roe brought out a revolutionary plane at this time; it was a monoplane with enclosed cockpit. The pilot having vision through windows of celluloid. To gain excess the pilot had to go through a trap door in the roof. This plane flew at Brooklands in 1912 and Roe decided that this was his entry for the competition. He was also keen to use a British engine; he discarded his French Gnome engine, in favour of a British 6O hp engine. Lieutenant Parke piloted Roe's plane. At the test it did all that was required except for one point and that was that it did not climb as required. This was because the prop could not take the full power of the engine, which had to be throttled back. The plane took nine minutes to do the climb instead of five. The full prize money was awarded to Colonel Cody an American who had lived in Britain for some years. This was his own construction with an American engine. Roe's machine performed impeccably but he got nothing. The British Government of the day gave little encouragement to their own air pioneers, this would be really important in the years to come.

Nothing knocked Verdon Roe out of his stride in his search for a good reliable machine. In 1912 he sold twelve standard Avro Bi-planes and his business began to prosper. On January 1st 1913, a firm called 'A.V. Roe & Company Limited' was formed with £30,000 capital. The money took no raising. For some reason shortly after, things got a little quiet, and there was some worry about the future of the company. Strangely, it was Germany who shook the company into life when they ordered a seaplane. This was new for Roe, and it made the War Office sit up and take notice, the First World War was only one year away and here was Germany purchasing an experimental seaplane.

By this time Roe had completed his 4th bi-Plane, which had its own cockpit for the pilot. Roe thought he would change the way he numbered his planes calling this particular one 'Avro 504', and this made a tremendous difference to his business. This plane was perfect and continued in production for eighteen years. During World War I, more than a thousand were built, initially as a reconnaissance plane, then as a bomber. In 1914 three Avros made a raid on a German Zeppelin shed at Friedrichshafen, on Lake Constance. The planes flew one hundred miles with four twenty-pound bombs on each plane. The Avro only had an 80 hp engine with top speed of 80mph. The planes released all of the bombs except for one, damaging the Zeppelin and blowing up a gas works. One Avro was shot down. The main job of the Avro plane was as a trainer as it was safe and reliable. Hundreds of Royal Flying Corps (later the Royal Air Force) pilots were trained on them, and. Prince Albert, later George VI earned his wings in an Avro 504.

After the war the industry slumped and Roe again found it hard going even in 1920. Roe manufactured planes for the times, producing inexpensive light aircraft. The most popular being the Avro Avian, an 80hp. engine getting a maximum speed of 100 mph and only costing £700. The Australian Bert Hinkler making the most of this wonderful plane, in 1928 completed a solo flight from London to Australia in fifteen days.

A.V. Roe pioneered as much as anyone but in 1928 he relinquished control when he was bought out by the Armstrong Whitworth Company, and in many ways he must of sighed a sigh of relief because of the trials a tribulations he suffered in his life – simply to keep his country to the fore in aviation. Alliott Verdon Roe risked his life, money and indeed his very existence to establish the British as leaders in the field of flight. No doubt planes such as the Lancaster, Vulcan, and the Avro Anson 500 series, all completed their parts in keeping this Country free from domination and persecution.

'PER ARDUA AD ASTRA'

Avro 621 Tutor:

Avro 504K

Avro Lancaster

War Time bomber crews during the war trusted the Lancaster to get them to missions and home once more; mechanically rarely letting them down. Below the 500 series of Avro Ansen played its roll as a quality plane, then after the war became a trusted commercial aero Plane.

Avro Ansen:

WILLIAM WILBERFORCE
(The man who freed slaves)

The Wilberforce family arrived at Beverley from Wilberforce, near York, in the mid seventeenth century. William Wilberforce was born in 1659. He had a business, which was part of the flourishing Baltic Trade and was situated at Kingston upon Hull, a few miles further south from Beverley. It was ironic at the time that Hull was the 4th port in England after London; and it was growing rich solely out of the profits from the slave trade. The other Ports, which gained from this appalling trade, were Liverpool and Bristol. William Wilberforce lived in a magnificent red brick mansion on the High Street. The front of this house overlooked the River Hull, where days were whiled away gazing at ships loading and unloading cargoes of hemp and timber from Riga and St. Petersburg and iron from Sweden. Many Yorkshire products were exported including, Sheffield cutlery and even ponies.

In no time at all William was an Alderman. He had a vigorous and exciting mind and could make money in the blink of an eye. He owned land in three parishes around Hull one area being inherited from his mother; this consisted of tenanted farms but had no Manor House. William Wilberforce married into the Thornton family, marrying Hannah, this family also prospered from the Baltic Trade.

Wilberforce in Early Life

Robert Wilberforce married Elizabeth Bird from London, and his sister married her brother. The Bird family was heavily into banking with premises in London and Hull. The third child, and only son of Robert and Hannah, they named William the subject of this story. He would be known throughout the world as *'The man who freed slaves'*.

William was born on 24th August 1659; he was blessed with many aunts, uncles, and sisters, all reasonably well off because of the astute business acumen of family interests around York and Hull. They were also indirectly connected to the slave trade as ports were flourishing because of this callous trade. William Wilberforce's father died aged 40 when he was only nine, and Abel Smith now

45

ran the Wilberforce business, renaming it, 'Wilberforce and Smith'. William, at this very young age, went to live with his aunt and uncle, William and Hannah, who had no children and who William adored. They would be his Guardians. William's new home was a Wimbledon Villa in the lovely Surrey countryside. Their second home was a large house at St. James Palace London. William attended boarding school at Putney where he did a little of most subjects, including arithmetic, writing, and reading. He wasn't much impressed with the school and looked forward to his vacations with his aunt and uncle. They took long walks in the Surrey countryside, and during these times they spoilt him a little, obviously because he was all the family they had. His Aunt Hannah was more afraid of William becoming a Methodist, as this religion was rife in this particular school. She was so worried that she took a coach to London and took him from the school and installed him in their grandfather's old school at Pocklington, at the foot of the Wolds, 13 miles from York. On a hill behind the village, 'York Minster' could be clearly seen.

Wilberforce & Education

William spent the following 5 years at Pocklington (1771-1776) as a boarder. The school was founded in 1514 and became a grammar school in the 20th Century accommodating 125 boys. At the age of 17 William went to Cambridge, entering St. John's College, which had links with Pocklington. Swatting and study were second place to playing cards and other pursuits and later William regretted not being made to buckle down with his studies. It took all of Wilberforce's quick intellect and talent, coupled with his magnificent memory, to get him through his examinations. Where he may have passed with honours – he barely scraped through. William loved entertaining and his unlimited funds allowed him to do this with ease. He enjoyed singing, listening to good conversation, and listening to instrumental music.

Pitt and Wilberforce – Friends in Politics:

William Wilberforce Snr. died in 1777 leaving the young William very rich indeed. It was inevitable that he would enter politics, and he entered the house before Pitt, in the spring of 1780. Wilberforce stood for Hull and the results went extraordinarily in his favour, polling twice as many votes as the other two together: Wilberforce, 1126; Manners 673; Hartley 453, Wilberforce and Manners being elected.

William made friends with Lake District people whom he met in the House, one being Wordsworth's uncle the other being brother to Fletcher Christian who led the mutiny against Bligh in the South Seas.

William Wilberforce never tired of the Lakes and called it England's paradise, he boated on Windermere, walked the fells, and had a seven year tenancy on a small Manor House, *'Rayrigg'*, situated right on the Lakeside. The Lakes brought

William his greatest friendship, with Colonel John Pennington; he was 30 years older than William and heir to Muncaster in Eskdale, which had magnificent views of Scafell from its terrace.

Early in June 1780, a mob from Hull, encouraged by the recent Gordon riots, burnt down the new Roman Catholic Chapel in Postern Gate. This was the first chapel built by Catholics since the reformation, and the result of hard work by this community. There was anti-popery fury in 1780 and this could be traced back to a limited Catholic Relief Bill, which Sir George Seville had introduced. There was also a little movement on anti-slavery and David Hartley an eccentric, and son of a philosopher put forward a motion in Parliament, this laid the foundation of the Extirpation of Slavery in England.

Hartley again attacked slavery and the general feeling at the time was that it was an unpleasant but a necessary trade. Hartley wore peculiar clothes and did not powder his hair; he secured his glasses by a band on the top of his head. Wilberforce, also having an eye problem, dressed strictly to the fashion of the day and used an eyeglass hung by a ribbon. Hartley's speeches were said to be long and dreary but he never missed a point. This was the start of Wilberforce's lifetime campaign against slavery and he contacted a friend, who at the time was in the West Indies, asking him to send him details of this formidable trade. Early in his school career at Pocklington, Wilberforce wrote to a York Paper deploring the odious traffic in human flesh.

William took his seat in St. Stephens Chapel, on the 31st October 1780, on the opposition backbenches, behind the speaker's chair. Pitt was defeated for a post at Cambridge University and entered the House in January. Pitt's maiden speech was brilliant and acclaimed by the whole House. Pitt was now Williams's closest friend. Wilberforce's first recorded speech was on the 17th May 1781, during the committee stage of a bill for preventing smuggling; he had presented a petition from Hull and spoke against spirits being confiscated from a ship carrying more than the permitted amount. During the recess in 1783, peace had been negotiated with France. Britain had been having sea victories and it looked a little like France was surrendering. Wilberforce was invited by Pitt to second the address to the Crown to ratify the treaty.

Prime Minister Pitt

During this period, a coalition in Parliament was not liked and the King offered the premiership to Pitt, who was not yet 24 – Pitt declined. At this time Pitt was Chancellor and resigned this post allowing the Fox/North coalition to succeed, and for a time Pitt was free of responsibility. Wilberforce could not match Pitt's lucidity and debating skills, but he ranged his eloquence at Pitt's side. The India Bill passed in the Commons but the Lords threw it out on the direct intervention of the King. *(The East India Company's possessions would have been ruled by a seven-man committee of coalition and would be open* to *corruption).* Next day, 18thDecember, the King dismissed the coalition and sent for Pitt who became Prime Minister at the age of 24 in a hostile Commons. Pitt did not dissolve Parliament, but consolidated his position not only in Parliament but also in the country. Wilberforce and Wyvill helped Pitt draw up a reform bill whereby the 35 boroughs with the smallest electorates would be bought up by consent, giving eventually 72 seats for re-distribution round London this included the large new towns of the industrial revolution. Wilberforce's speech on the 18th April showed that he already disliked party politics, by destroying the 'Rotten Boroughs', which were used by powerful men to control votes in the House, freedom of speech would be restored and the party connections would vanish. He wished to register a vote divest of any sentiments of attachments. Wilberforce never thought of himself a party man and certainly not a Tory. He was a Pitite, believing in Pitt's Policies.

William Wilberforce was then living at Scarborough, but moved near to Nottingham and stayed a long time with Samuel Smith's family, where they had a new mansion. Here Wilberforce decided to educate himself further and read history, economics, literature, and philosophy. The bible became his favourite book and he learned passages by heart. William made himself personal rules and generally broke them in venal matters. He had a charming inability to live up to rigid standards and failings kept him human. Wilberforce was never far away from slavery and Ramsey, a well known campaigner and writer, wrote and published a long essay on the treatment of slaves in the British Colonies. He had been urged to do this by Lady Middleton and Bishop Porteus, he proposed steps of total emancipation and said that free labour would yield more profit for plantation owners. Other books were written regarding the slave trade attacking it for its barbarous cruelty and oppression. Wilberforce was now fully committed to an assault on the slave trade, nothing but the complete abolition of this horrifying trade would do. Thirty years later he stressed this in a letter he sent to Quaker Joseph Gurney. The immediate aim was to stop the supply of the slaves; this would both force the planters to treat their present slaves better and as irreplaceable stock. Robert Norris, a trader and traveller of the day, said that most slaves were criminals and had escaped the gallows. Wilberforce hoped abolition might come swiftly and by international agreement. William Eden, who Pitt had sent to Paris with the rank of Minister, to negotiate the advantageous commercial treaty with France, was asked by Wilberforce to sound out the French on the subject of Slaves. William told Eden that the manual export from the west coast of Africa, by all nations, exceeded 100,000; small numbers were criminals and prisoners of war. Wilberforce further informed him that the arrival of the slaves in the West Indies was no less than barbarous; he also said that on many estates the numbers of slaves was maintained by breeding.

Wilberforce continued gathering evidence, he did, however, realize just what he was up against. This had been a way of life and many powerful traders who would stop at nothing to carry on with this uncouth business opposed him. It had been their source of wealth for centuries the date for Wilberforce's motion was early February 1788. This date proved impracticable, but he still hoped it could be produced in 5 or 6 weeks. Wilberforce took ill, the pressures of the abolition bill was enormous and would have beaten any lesser man than William.

Objectors had to be heard by counsel at the Bar of the House, Wilberforce also had to brief counsel for cross-examination of witnesses. A week later on, 19th February, William was overcome by sheer exhaustion, fever and loss of appetite this together with many sleepless nights. Wilberforce consulted his doctor, James Pitcairn, the Scottish physician, who had a good reputation in London. He did not help William at all, so he confined himself to bed. Pitt urged William to get a little country air at Clapham, where he had a room. He returned the following day a little better and his doctor told him to drink the waters of Bath. Before setting out for Bath, he had a complete relapse on the 8th March, with the same symptoms as before only this time he had diarrhea it pointed to ulcerative colitis caused by stress. Lord Muncaster and Matthew Montague took on the job as nurses, his mother was also sent for. Doctor Richard Warren, who treated the Prince of Wales and later would make more money than any other physicians in the country –although he had predicted that the King would not recover from his 'madness'. Warren also said of Wilberforce "That little fellow with his calico gut, cannot possibly survive twelve months". A combination of Warren and Dr Willis went further saying, "Wilberforce did not have the stamina to last a fortnight". William finally got over the crisis and Warren got the benefit of it. Warren and Pitcairn ordered William to take an 18th Century cure all, which was Opium. Bob Smith *(Lord Carrington)* commented later that his health was restored by that what should have destroyed him using opium in large quantities. *[Opium was usually administered in the liquid form of Laudanum; Warren gave Wilberforce the drug in pill form. On modern day thinking, Opium would be ideal for Wilberforce's condition because of the stress element.)*

Pitt postponed the debate on the Wilberforce Bill until he gathered further strength.

The First Reading of the Bill for the Abolition of Slavery:

The Bill was eventually debated and William gave a three and a half hour speech. The speech was free from rhetoric or bitterness. He was easy on the slave owners saying they did not mean to be cruel; he dealt with the arguments of opposition efficiently. He then proposed his twelve resolutions. Pitt said later that this was an error of judgment, having brought the house to a pitch. Lord Penrhyn and the member for Liverpool, accused Wilberforce of misrepresentation and Alderman Nathaniel Newnham *(a former Lord Mayor of London)* who incidentally had extensive sugar refineries forecast the ruin of the city if the abolishment of slavery was passed.

Most of the House was still uneasy, obviously swayed by Wilberforce's facts put forward so shrewdly, yet worried in case it would cause economic disaster. The House formed a committee and heard more evidence on nine days of the summer, and then they adjourned until the next session. The date was 23 June, 1789 at the commencement of the new session, his opponents tried everything they knew to stop Wilberforce, even requesting the House not to allow him to move the Bill, because of the time taken up by cross-questioning witnesses. Wilberforce ingeniously outflanked his opponents by having these witnesses cross-questioned by a select committee upstairs. Spring passed to summer, witnesses representing the trade and those against were heard. The transcripts numbered ten thousand folio pages *[All apparently burned in the fire of 1834]*. The year was 1790 and Pitt decided to go to the Country a year before he needed to. William Wilberforce would soon find out if his causes outside Yorkshire had cost him his seat. In the recess, Wilberforce carried out his constituency duties as a good MP should, presenting petitions putting forward people for promotion in the Armed Services. Wilberforce especially liked interceding on behalf of convicts, and if it was possible, to save them from the gallows or Botany Bay, he did. In one case a convict named 'Sheperdson', condemned to the Hulks, he asked if he might have a slightly more merciful punishment of compulsory enlistment on a man-of-war. Wilberforce even looked up the Judge's remarks at the time of the sentencing sending them to Scrope Bernard MP, under secretary at the Home Office, to have Lord Grenville urgently review the case, in this particular case it was unsuccessful.

General Election 1790

The General Election was held in June 1790. In William's county it showed Duncomb and Wilberforce favourites and they were returned without the expense of a poll. At this time Wilberforce had a bad carriage accident at Bridlington, this seemed to have affected his nerves later in life. He hoped to be able resume the select committee at once and he hoped that Pitt would allow the slave trade precedence over the budget debates. As it was, the select committee delayed its hearings until February 1791. There was also news of an abortive slave rebellion in the West Indies, where *'Massa King Wilberforce'*, says they should work only a three-day week for full pay.

Wilberforce was again very much up against it during this time. He was encouraged by *[very much used]* words, in a letter from John Wesley. He wrote,

50

'*God has raised you up for this* very *thing, you will be worn out by the opposition of men and Devils... But if* God *be for you, who can be against you.*' Wesley wrote this when he was eighty-seven, the day before the onset of his brief and final illness. (*The letter of John Wesley 'to a member of parliament', was probably written to Beaufoy).* Wilberforce greatly admired the Wesley's and actually met both John and Charles. Charles Wesley's widow and unmarried daughter were on reduced circumstances. He asked Hannah Moore to investigate. Wilberforce and two friends provided an annuity for Mrs. Wesley in August 1792, which shamed the Methodist movement into raising another. At last the debate came, Abolition of Slavery 2nd reading. On 18th April 1791. A speaker in support of abolition, James Martin Tewkesbury, sounded a truly humane religious Christian.

Philip Francis brought out two further instances of cruelty. The debate continued on Thursday, Sir William Young thought it would lead to the loss of the Colonies. He agreed abolition must come, but other nations would seize England's share. Matthew Montague uttered a burst in Wilberforce's favour saying, 'is that any reason why we all should be guilty of murder'. Late in the debate Pitt spoke emphasizing the injustice and 'impolicy' of the slave trade. Fox made a brilliant speech saying that if the house voted no, it would give parliamentary sanction to rapine, robbery and murder.

The debate continued all night. On the morning of 20th April 1791, Wilberforce made a brief and short reply to the debate. The House divided and there was about 50% present to vote. Sir William Dolben as Chairman could not vote, he sadly recorded on his manuscript the figures, 'No's 163, Yes 88, majority against abolition, 75. In 1792 Dundas put forward an amendment whereby the slave trade would be gradually abolished, this to take effect in seven years and roughly at the turn of the century. This was carried by 230 votes to 85. England went to war with France. Wilberforce was not a pacifist; he once was asked to join a pacifist movement but refused, saying that the scriptures allowed defensive wars. Wilberforce in fact hated the war for many reasons but mainly because it would slow down his slavery bill,

Barbara Spooner

After she wrote to Wilberforce in 1797, requesting spiritual guidance from William, he met her on April 15th, falling head over heels in love. Barbara Spooner was the third of ten children of Isaac Spooner, a rich elderly, banker, merchant and Iron Master from Birmingham, living at Elmdon Hall, and having a second house at Bath. Barbara was gay, good-humoured, and very pretty.

It was at this time that Wilberforce received details of a mutiny in the navy at Spithead; Wilberforce knew the sailors' feelings because of poor pay and conditions. Admiral Middleton hated the system of the press gang, which created

51

discontent from the start. In 1756 there was a mutiny on *'HMS Culloden'*, he threatened to sink her and this ultimately solved the crisis. There was discontent throughout the navy at this time. The fleet had also mutinied at Nore. Wilberforce could not get Barbara out of his mind, it was affecting his eating and sleeping, so much so that he threw caution to the wind and wrote to Barbara and her family requesting her hand in marriage. The marriage of William and Barbara took place on Tuesday morning 30th May 1797. It was a quiet wedding at the parish church of Walcott, Bath, the bridegroom being thirty-eight and the bride twenty.

Wilberforce bought Broomfield, the house had a long drive with an avenue of young trees, and it was four miles from Westminster Bridge and a mile and a half from Battersea Footbridge. Barbara had problems with their first child, William, who was born 21st July 1798 and would bring them much unhappiness. Wilberforce was a doting father and he approved his wife's determination to breast-feed the babies. Barbara's protectiveness of William prolonged his life.

Duel of Honour

Duelling in Parliament those days was important, not unlike France and also Germany. On Whit Sunday, 1798, Pitt and George Tierney fought a duel on Putney Heath. Tierney had placed himself into the opposition leadership when Fox and his friends came out of the Commons under a cloud. Dudley Ryder acted as Pitt's second and the Speaker watched seated on a horse. Pitt fired his second shot into the air and the duellists, unarmed, travelled back in the same coach. Pitt and Tierney had insulted each other in the house. Pitt tall as a beanpole and Tierney having a huge frame. The duel shocked Wilberforce very much, that a Prime Minister of the day could fight a duel this way. He questioned the 'Honour' when a gentleman was hindered from telling unpleasant truths to another because 'Honour', forbade refusal of the challenge, which might follow. Wilberforce tabled a motion outlawing duelling but had to withdraw it as Pitt threatened to resign because of his recent escapade.

Continuation of the War

Pitt attempted to end the war with France but was unsuccessful and Wilberforce, from then on, supported the war wholeheartedly. Britain fought for its very existence, as France broke off the second round of secret peace talks in 1797. They also smashed all the Continental Allies and now Britain stood alone against the brilliant military mind of all- conquering Napoleon Bonaparte. There was also the great worry of an invasion by the French – there had already been incursions into Ireland and an attempt on Wales.

These were the years of great Generals and Admirals in particular the Duke of Wellington and Lord Nelson with his sea victories at St. Vincent and the destruction of the French fleet on the Nile. This was also the year that Captain

Bligh returned to the South Seas after the mutiny on the Bounty. Wilberforce and Admiral Middleton secured passages for two missionaries to Tahiti, but they withdrew before the ship sailed, the Missionary Society responsible for these two, attempted to get Wilberforce to be president of their organization but he declined. It was a known fact that Wilberforce, up to the time of his marriage, gave half of his income to worthy charities and good causes.

Wilberforce starts a Family

Wilberforce sat gazing over Bognor Rocks *[Not yet Bognor Regis]* he was now forty-one; the date was 24th August 1800. He prayed that he might live a life more honourable to God and useful to man *('that I may bear about with me, a sense of thy presence').* Days later, his wife now pregnant became nervous and irritable losing her appetite. She also had a high temperature. The doctors diagnosed Typhoid. Five days later William was able to inform her father, Isaac Spooner, that Barbara was improving – although she still had fever. Barbara bore Elizabeth safely and over the next seven years a further three children, it was said that her general health never recovered from the Typhoid problem of 1800.

Catholic Emancipation

This was the period of Pitt's crisis with the King over Catholic Emancipation. Pitt knew that Roman Catholics had had a raw deal for years for recognizing the start of Christianity as being St **Peter** *[Thou art Peter* **(The Rock) and upon this rock I shall build my Church]**. Wilberforce looked favourably on union with Ireland and had wanted admission of Roman Catholics to Parliament even before Pitt. The King refused to agree with emancipation and Pitt resigned, when the King secured Speaker Paddington to form a Ministry. One way or another Catholic Emancipation would again re-surface as Catholicism at the time was treated very unfairly. The slave Abolition Bill started to again come to life and Wilberforce was glad.

Continuation of the War

Wilberforce insisted that as Britain conquered colonies that the abolition became law in their constitution. Pitt found himself very much back at the helm; these were crucial times and needed the guidance and talent of such a statesman. The Napoleonic war on land and sea was at its height, especially the 'Rochefort Squadron' in the West Indies. British Men of War could not be deflected to enforce an order in Council against their own merchantmen. Wilberforce thought that the autumn of 1805 would see the climax of the sea war. Pitt appointed Lord Melville as first Lord of the Admiralty, but he had to resign because he had been party to gross dishonesty in this department. Pitt was very upset about this but quickly appointed the incorruptible Sir Charles Middleton as First Sealord. Strategic and administrative skill, along with a little tact, was needed at this time and Middleton seemed the man for the job. In the early hours of a November morning in 1805 word was received that Britain had gained a complete victory at Trafalgar, but Lord Nelson was dead. Britain was now in complete control of the seas and it would have a profound effect on the slave trade and abolition. In January 1806, Pitt died, mostly from a broken heart from the loss of Lord Nelson, whose glorious victory, especially at Trafalgar, tipped the scales in Britain and Pitt's way. Wilberforce had lost a dear and great friend who had stood by him in his fight for abolition, especially with his tactful help in presenting the bill at the best times.

Pitt's Funeral

Wilberforce attempted to pay off Pitt's debts by private subscription, rather than having the controversy of public subscription. Pitt's funeral service was held at Westminster Abbey. Charles Villiers carried the crest of Pitt, and Wilberforce was in support. Wilberforce thought long and hard after the death of William Pitt, mainly about the final stages of the Abolition Bill. He was reassured when Lord Grenville was elected Prime Minister and Fox became Foreign Secretary. The Bill was progressed passed from the Commons to the Lords, Fox and Grenville backing it all the way. Fox became seriously ill, he had dropsy and his very life was in danger. Wilberforce looked back on the years he had attended Parliament with Fox, his arguments for and against issues, he stood staunchly behind the Abolition bill. William worried that if Fox died the bill may not be consummated in 1807, after partial abolition in 1806.

Wilberforce left his troubles behind him and went to Lyme Regis, where Barbara loved swimming in the sea and where he could be with his children. He also had heavy correspondence to answer and was also working on a book on the Abolition of Slavery. Grenville and Fox now decided to have a General Election. There was a danger that Wilberforce may lose his seat, as Walter Fawkes of Farnley would stand in opposition against him and Lascelles – he was worried about the final stages of the Bill.

Wilberforce hurried to Yorkshire giving speeches as he went. He need not have worried, they carried him shoulder high to the meeting rooms and it was obvious that they admired him as much as always, and even more so on becoming aware of his campaign for the freedom of the slaves was reaching its conclusion. At Sheffield and Leeds the crowds were also very enthusiastic. Wilberforce was elected easily but Fawkes was preferred to Lascelles. Wilberforce's political knowledge would again be there as a guiding influence in these trying years when the Abolition Bill reached its final stage. He now concentrated on his book; it had taken no less than six years to complete. It was said that new Prime Minister Grenville had said in the Commons that Wilberforce's Bill must be backed in total but not a penny of Treasury money must be used. Subscriptions came from everywhere, the Methodists and Church

54

Evangelicals, several Peers and Magnates all were in support, saying that Wilberforce was a true Independent. Funds were just not a problem to get rid of this ghastly trade. Charles James Fox died just prior to the Election after serving over forty years in Parliament. His predecessors did well in the Election to follow.

Lord Grenville moved the second reading of the Bill with a glorious speech and the House sat all night, with the Duke of Clarence defending the trade Lord Eldon also came out strongly against the Bill. The Admiral, the Earl of St. Vincent said that Grenville must have been charmed into backing the Bill by a witch doctor and that he was not aware of the damage he was doing. The Peers divided themselves at 5 am. And the vote count was 100 to 36 a majority of 64 in favour of the Bill. Next evening the Committee stage was passed swiftly. Bishops of Durham and London shook Wilberforce's hand warmly the majority of other Peers did the same? Most speeches supported the Bill wholeheartedly as one member sat down six or even eight were on their feet. The House rose almost to a man turning towards Wilberforce cheering. Wilberforce sat with a bowed head tears streaming down his face, he replied briefly to the debate.

Abolition of the Slave Trade Law

Young Earl Percy *[Northumberland Heir)* proposed that slavery should be immediately abolished; the House sensed a red herring and called loudly 'Question'. Percy sat down and the House divided, Ayes 283, No's *16*, majority in favour of the abolition of slavery was an amazing 267. *'What's next,'* Wilberforce laughingly remarked to Thornton *'the Lottery?'* It was certainly on the list. The bill came up for its third reading on 16th March and passed unopposed. On the morning of 23rd March, Wilberforce was informed that a clerical error was found in one of the amendments to be laid before the Lords that afternoon. The Lords had to correct it before it could be debated in the Commons. The procedure was agreed in the Lords, receiving protest from Westmoreland, and the following day the amendment was corrected and agreed. Grenville had already received the Royal assent for the Bill, also two minor ones. They were actually the last acts of his administration. The date was Wednesday the 25th March 1807. The Bill for the Abolition of the Slave Trade became law; the problems were now to enforce it.

Lord Castlereagh began to surface as a leading member of the House, when he was War Minister in 1809, he challenged Canning to a duel on Putney Heath, because of facts learned from Lord Camden, and they shot at each other. Later, in 1811, Castlereagh was leader of the House. Canning although a talented Politician would not work with Castlereagh at all sacrificing his political career.

Catholic Emancipation

The intransigence of George III and the fall of Pitt changed the attitude concerning Catholic Emancipation in 1813. Wilberforce felt that the time was right to again debate this problem, even though he was still against the grant to 'Maynooth College' for the training of priests. Wilberforce had a lower opinion of 'Political Protestant' men who had no religion yet belaboured Roman Catholics for political ends. The anti- Romanists of the day Patrick Duigenan was being conferred with a Privy Councillorship. Duigenan with his bob wig and Connemara stockings was laughed at in the Commons, but his ideas on Catholicism at the time were obnoxious.

To Wilberforce, religion was too sacred to be a political toy. Wilberforce began to mistrust a system whereby the Catholic Community, which in England was still numerical small, had to be represented by Protestants. He refused to look at Roman Catholics as being sinister. Wilberforce thought that they would become less vocal once they had representatives of their own faith. For all this he was still undecided on whether to admit Roman Catholics to Parliament. By 6th March 1813, he was clear in his mind on the Catholic problem when he unequivocally recommended the abolition of Penal Statutes in matters of Religion.

Enforcing Abolition

Castlereagh at last produced a treaty with Spain in September 1817, immediately abolishing the slave trade north of a line, with in three years to the south. The Spanish treaty allowed British cruisers to search suspected vessels for slaves and if there were slaves on board, the ship could be seized. Sierra-Leone muddled its way forward there were 10,000 free Negroes, most being rescued from holds of ships. Most were now experiencing the civil rights of a British Colony. '*H.M.S. Derwant*' brought into Sierra Leone 167 blacks from a seized cargo ship, conforming to the abolition act and providing the prize money, which the navy traditionally received from every capture – be it a 100-gun man of war or a slave ship.

Lake District

Wilberforce turned his attention to his family and Barbara he decided to take them on the long promised holiday to the Lake District. The year was 1818. Wilberforce had Southey looking for houses in Keswick, but he changed his mind and sought out Dorothy and William Wordsworth, who found two small houses at Rydal near Ambleside. Wilberforce brought five of their seven servants who were bedded down in the village. The full party to the Lake District numbered nineteen plus the horses. The two girls Barbara 19, and Lizzie 17, looked unaffected by all the fuss, exactly as young educated ladies should look. Wilberforce was still travelling with the two youngest children. His carriage arrived and there was an emotional meeting. Dorothy had not seen William for twenty-five years and his body had aged somewhat, but he was still stronger than he looked. He was able to walk up Skiddaw, getting wet in the process. He was also capable of walking many miles especially in the Lakes. The older boys walked a great deal in the fells. Robert and Samuel returned to school

William Wilberforce Junior

William returned to Trinity for his second year. He was not studying correctly at College and he had, unknown to Wilberforce, purchased a second horse at a high price – when his father was trying to cut expenses. He allowed other boys to take advantage of his weaknesses, especially being Wilberforce's son, he was also telling lies. William had also been drunk at home when Blundell, Wilberforce's great friend lay dead in the next room. William was suspended from Trinity and this pulled on the heartstrings of Wilberforce. Williams's horse was also confiscated and Wilberforce stopped him from coming home, this action nearly breaking Wilberforce's, heart. William took it well and his love grew for his father with discipline. Young William did not return to Trinity but read at the Bar in the care of John Owen (secretary of the Bible Society). The following year William married Owens's beautiful daughter; who did not have a penny in the world, on the 13th August 1822. The following year, 1823 Lord Canning became neighbours to Wilberforce.

Final Thoughts

During the year, 1823-24, Wilberforce suffered from colds and flu in the chest, the following day his old bowel problem returned. Three schemes drew his attention, creation of the National Gallery, the establishment of the Trustee Savings Bank, and an act against cruelty to animals. Wilberforce talked about things in heaven and on earth, and he was still very alert. He remarked, after hearing the Abolition Bill had passed its final stage on 26th July 1833, that he had lived to witness the day that England had given twenty million sterling for the Abolition of slavery. On Saturday he suddenly grew tired and his mind was quiet and tranquil. On Sunday he fainted and deteriorated rapidly, at 3 am Monday 29th July 1833, William passed quietly away from this life.

On Saturday 3rd August, thousands of Londoners wore mourning. Wilberforce's coffin entered Westminster Abbey. Two Royal Dukes, the Lord Chancellor, the Speaker and four Peers supported the Pall. Members of both houses walked in the procession. Apart from the choir it was a very plain funeral but exceptionally well attended.

William Wilberforce:

William Pitt the younger; great friend of Wilberforce and a brilliant Prime minister:

John Wesley, leader of Methodism. He was admired by Wilberforce; his words ('If God is for you –who can be against') comforted Wilberforce and kept him going to get his law on slavery passed:

Houses of Parliament London

SIR JOSEPH WILSON SWAN
(Inventor of the incandescent lamp)

Early Life

Joseph Swan was born on the Eve of all Hallows in 1828, at Sunderland. His father, John, and his mother, Isabella Swan, both of Scottish descent, settled in Durham in the middle of the 19th. Century. Their Ancestors were strong Yeoman farmer stock cross-bred with sea faring folk and known to be healthy because of the bracing sea air close to Bishop Wearmouth. It was probably a misfortune that stopped John Swan furthering a career as a seaman. John's father had owned his own Merchant ship and had died at sea. John's mother feared for her son's life – he being her only son, so John found himself shore based with a comfortable but interesting life, manufacturing and selling ship's anchors and heavy chains.

John still loved the sea and, having an inventive, mind devised nautical appliances like an anchor with moveable flukes, a life saving raft, and launching apparatus, also a signalling invention for giving warning in fog at sea. John did, however, make many sea voyages when he was involved in the transport of family goods. On one occasion acting as captain. Later in his life, with Captain Wiggins of *(Kara Sea Fame,* they chartered a ship and sailed to Iceland to collect a cargo of sheep. The voyage was taken too late in the year and when the sea was at its roughest. They picked up too many sheep and they had to be jettisoned in the rough weather on their return. John Swan was not an ideal businessman he was too easygoing and generous, always ready to help others. He was forever looking for new ideas losing money every time. Although his family never inherited money or goods what they did inherit from John Swan was generosity gentleness, integrity, enterprise, good brains, and finally, good constitutions. By 1820 John Swan had married Isabella daughter of George Cameron *(a member of the Cameron Clan who's forbears had settled at Esh, Co. Durham).* George Cameron was a stonemason and master builder, who established himself in early

58

life. He built the Old Exchange *(now a seaman's Institute)* still standing at High Street Sunderland. He was killed when a wall fell on him in a great storm in 1814.

Sunderland

John and Isabella first lived at Low Street Sunderland, where John was in business. Their house backed onto the River Wear and his young wife could hear the regular beatings and floggings of the sailors on the Men o' War on the river. After the birth of Elizabeth, their daughter, they moved to Pallion Hall, a large house with a garden sloping to the Wear. The house was two miles upstream from Sunderland. It was at the Hall that two sons were born John and Joseph. There were many happy memories of their young lives here. At the opposite side of the river shipbuilding was progressing. Steam Boats were relatively new, and they were cautiously experimenting with them. All of the ships to this period were wood; thoughts of steel floating seemed a long way off.

The young family quickly developed, Joseph in particular took an interest in most things. The family life was glorious and happy, the parent's happiness shone through to the children. The following three lines of a Wesleyan Hymn epitomizes what the children thought,

"…and then we'll shout and sing, and make the pallion arches ring when all the swans come home…'

This happiness lasted throughout the children's lives, later there was a downturn and John Swan moved his family to a smaller house at Olive Street, Sunderland. The family now consisted of four boys and four girls. The children were sent to the best schools possible and Joseph had vivid memories of his school days. One person in particular was an old Captain, Commander John Kirtley RN. Who had fought with distinction under Nelson?" Kirtley called Joseph 'Ganymede'. Each day after his mid day meal, Joseph brought him his glass of *'Shrub'*, and also his yard long Turkish pipe with shag and aniseed. When Kirtley fell asleep Joseph spread the Gaud gossamer bandanna over his face, keeping silent until he again woke.

Close by the house was a Blacksmiths where the Allison's *(father & son)* carried on their work with the hammer and white-hot bar. There was also a carpenter's shop near-by where Joseph learned the use of the plane, mallet, and chisel. Joseph was very inquisitive, learning quickly how horses were shod, cows milked, how grass and hay were cut and stacked and how the wheat harvest was gathered. Men and woman with sickles *('Shear low down')* the farmer saying. Joseph knew all about birds their nests and eggs. The flowery banks near to the sea, the sweet meadows with cow slips and primroses. The hedges, which later were thick with wild roses. Joseph knew the arts of the cobblers and tailors, how nails were made and candles too. The chandler dipping the blanched frame from which the wicks were hung into the bad smelling fat. The long steel bars were observed being converted into nails of mixed sizes. The making of pottery and glass and also the brickfield was visited, where woman carried bricks from the moulding table. Joseph watched hemp being heckled and spun into rope yarn and finally made into ships cables.

One of Joseph's uncles was a rope-maker, and it was here that he broadened his knowledge of this mysterious craft. It was also here that Joseph learned all about boilers and steam engines, learning how gas was produced and how corn was milled. On Queen Victoria's Coronation day, these same gas works for the first time provided gas illumination. The rope maker uncle, was Robert Cameron of Esh, he was also an inventor and was awarded a prize for an improved lifeboat and machinery for rope making. Joseph, after a period going from one interest to another, joined a school run by three old ladies, the Misses Herries who were sisters. Their father lived with them and looked no older than his daughters. Joseph stayed at school for about two years, where he learned to read and spell. He also learned to knit, darn and stitch. This was the time that Joseph acquainted himself with an electrical machine owned by Mr. John Ridley, a friend of the family who later invented a reaping machine used in Australia.

Joseph's brother had been sent to a large boys' school, kept by Dr. Wood at Hendon Lodge. Joseph joined his brother at the school and they were inseparable calling each other Castor and Pollox, there were two hundred other boys at the school. Hendon Hall was an old Mansion with extensive grounds, which were used for boys' games. Joseph stayed for two years, after this the school removed to Hylton Castle, famous for its ghost *'the cauld lad of Hylton'*. He was a servant boy who was murdered by his master, one of the Barons of Hylton, in a fit of passion. The boys left school together, John being fourteen, Joseph not yet thirteen. What they learned at school did not amount to much, Joseph learned more out of school than in. Two books that Joseph did remember with pleasure were *'Ewing's Elements of Elocution'*, this contained good literature, prose and verse. Joseph obtained his original love of poetry from this book. The other book, which inspired Joseph, was a little book of *'Rudimentary Chemistry,'* written by Hugo Reid, which had a large influence on Joseph Swan's mind. Joseph learned the workings of gunpowder early in his life; having a relative as a druggist he had access to any of the raw material he required. The Swan family fortunes were on a downturn about this time, mainly due to their father over generosity when backing friend's bills and over considering his workers interests. Joseph went to live with Captain Kirtley at Elswick; who had taken a father-like interest in him. In the autumn of 1842 he returned to Sunderland where he was articled as an apprentice druggist with 'Hudson and Osbaldiston'; his term was six years. Prior to the completion of his apprenticeship Joseph became free after both partners died. This opened the way for him to join John Mawson in his Chemist and druggist business at Newcastle. Joseph became a member of Sunderland Athenaeum and with it access to a good library, where he studied scientific books and journals of the day. Among others the following interested him most, *'The Edinburgh and Dublin Philosophical Magazine'*, quite a new publication, *'The Electrical Magazine'*, edited by *C. V. Walker*, the *'Repertory of Patent Inventions'*, interested him together with Star's *'Incandescent Electric Lamp'*, which was patented in England in 1845. It consisted of a short carbon pencil operating in a vacuum above a column of mercury. Several were exhibited in London but they were not a commercial success as they quickly blackened. It was however an incandescent, and the beginning of the electric light.

Joseph Swan attended many lectures over the following three years at Carlisle and at Newcastle. At one lecture a principle of electric lighting by means of a piece of *'Iridio-platinum'* wire was considered. The speaker, Richardson, also lectured on the same principle at the Athenaeum at Sunderland. This laid the seed in Swan's mind remembering to avoid fuse wire, and later the idea germinated. Daniel's battery had just been invented and this developed into Electro Plating, then eventually into Electro-Metallurgy. Joseph noticed in a shop window of Mr. Robson, a well-known engraver, of Bridge Street, Sunderland, a photographic self portrait *(Daguerreotype)*. Joseph came back often to view this portrait and fixed it firmly in his mind, the year was 1845. Photography from that moment became popular much the same as Electro-typing. Bingham wrote a book *'Daguerreotype Manipulation';* these were newly discovered arts and those who were interested were very excited with the progress in this area

Newcastle

Joseph Swan moved to Newcastle in 1846 when he was eighteen. He joined his friend and future brother in law, John Mawson, who had started a Chemist-druggist business on the *'Side'*, they then moved to *'Mosley Street'*, where the business became, *'Mawson & Swan'*. John Mawson was well thought of where ever he went; when still a young man he stood surety for a friend who defaulted and Mawson became liable for payment. At the time he was not able to discharge the payment and became bankrupt, but later he paid all of the creditors. This stood him in good stead and in later life he became Sheriff of Newcastle, and this was the man who Joseph Swan was fortunate to be associated with. Joseph became an asset to the business, especially when chemical manufacturers needed technical data. Mawson allowed Joseph to further his ideas, these were the days of *'Felice Orsini'*, who escaped from an Austrian prison and stayed in Blaydon. He charmed the ladies and had a wonderful voice. His life came to a violent end in 1858 when attempting to assassinate Napoleon III. Swan worked way into the night at their photographic studio in Mosley Street, apprentice Thomas Barclay helped him. Swan focused on producing permanent photographic prints free from fading. This was perfected in 1864 with the *'Carbon Process'*. Swan during 1855-56 got a serious infection of the lungs after experimenting with chemicals, he was sent to Rothsay in the isle of Bute, where in the west coast air his lungs healed. Joseph became acquainted with a young lady from Liverpool. She was vivacious and had a good sense of humour, she was a teacher called Fanny. On occasions she visited Newcastle and in 1861 became engaged to Joseph and in 1862 they married at Camberwell Chapel. In 1863 a son Cameron was born and in 1864 a daughter Mary Edmonds. The family moved to Leazes Terrace, Newcastle, where in April 1866, Joseph Henry was born. With regard to the *'Carbon Process'* swan paid his first visit to the Continent in July 1867. He took his wife and they visited Germany, Switzerland and France. At the end of the year they were honoured by the birth of twins

Sorrow

A large amount of Nitro-glycerin was found in a stable in Newcastle, and John Mawson, as High Sheriff, had the job to dispose of it and it was decided to bury it on the Town Moor. Before it could be disposed of it exploded killing everyone and fatally injuring Mawson. Everyone was full of grief and none more than Joseph Swan, who was left with the full responsibility of the business on his shoulders. He made the widowed Elizabeth a partner, giving her the wage that John would have earned. It would also create an interest for her. There was further grief for Joseph Swan in that his wife passed away, perhaps brought on by the death of John Mawson, the twins joined their mother in death shortly after.

Photographic Carbon Process

At the end of 1858, Swan experimented with the Carbon Process. He formed relief picture whose surface contour perfectly corresponded to the light and shades of silver print. His first attempt to carry out the idea consisted of a coating of a plate of glass with a mixture of lamp black solution of Gum Arabic and a solution of Bichromate of Potash. He exposed the plate when dry, in a camera with the uncoated surface of the glass turned towards the light, passing through a negative lens. The plate was then washed with water to remove the back of the sensitive coating, those portions of the film, which the light had not rendered insoluble. The experiment, though right in principle, was not a success because of insufficient exposure and it was not perfected until 1864. They achieved it by separating altogether the film and paper during the initial stages. Swan patented his Carbon Process in 1864 *(Patent No. 503)*. The Half-Tone process for making Typographical Blocks is in use today to illustrate books, magazines and newspapers and is the outcome of Swans inventions. Patents covering these were registered 6th July 1865 and 22nd July, Patent Nos. 1791 & 2969.

Joseph Swan devoted the next few years after the death of John Mawson in 1867, on organizing his business, focusing on photography. This led to a further discovery for Swan in *(Bromide Paper printing)* printing by artificial light, which was patented by Swan in 1879 no. 2968 and is still in universal use today. Swan for a while stayed on at Leazes Terrace with his wife's two sisters Maria and Hannah, who stayed to look after the older children. The twin boys only survived their mother by a few months. All of the stress of recent times told on Joseph's strength, health and spirits. He suffered from intense weariness and also of not fulfilling a duty. In June 1869 he went to the Lakes for a well-earned rest with special friends like John Hancock, the Northumbria naturalist, who was a pupil of Thomas Bewick. His intimate knowledge of birds and every form of wild life was just amazing and the rambles with him in the Lakes were tremendous. Swan himself was a great naturalist. The beauty of natural forms, colours and sounds filled him with pleasure if not rapture. His favourite poets were Shakespeare and Tennyson. In the summer of 1869 he moved from Newcastle to Low Fell, Gateshead, saying 'we live too long in smoke and anxieties, which robs the body of its natural nourishment'. It was with mixed feelings he left the old house, which had so many sad and happy memories.

Their new house was *'Underhill'*, which had a good garden overlooking the Ravensworth countryside and the valleys of the Tyne. Several other members of the family lived in the area, which was then a little village, set among green fields; the family was very close if not clannish. All of this time the business of *'Mawson & Swan'* was progressing; they further acquired a stationery and book selling business, formally run by Marston of Grey Street. Thomas Morgan, a very able Irishman, managed this and from time to time pictures appeared on show at the shop. At the time there was no art gallery in Newcastle.

Swan was considering marrying Hannah White, who was his sister-in-law. She had kept house after his wife's death. There was a problem at the time as it was classed as illegal to marry one's sister-in-law. Even though this was being debated in Parliament at that time. They also considered the children and Swan hoped that as the children grew they would have the same happy memories as he had. He regularly read to them passages from *'Canterbury Tales'*, *the idylls of the King'*, *and the 'Day Dream'*, and *'Young Lochinvar'*.

In the summer of 1871, *'Underhill'*, was closed for a time owing to an outbreak of Smallpox. The children and aunts were sent to Moffat and Keswick. Swan, after a short visit to the Lakes, remained at Gateshead staying at *'Ash field'*, in Gateshead the Mawson's home. The Bill for legalizing his marriage to his sister-in-law failed to pass and they consequently decided to marry in

Switzerland, leaving England in September 9th 1871. The marriage took place at the Reformed Church, Neufchatel on October 3rd 1871. They returned via Paris, where there was evidence of the siege during the Commune, and they were present during the trial of Rossel, an idealist leader of the Communists. *[Rossel with two other Communist leaders, Ferre & Bourgeois was sentenced to death and subsequently shot in the presence of 3000 soldiers on November 28th 1871].* The marriage was very happy and Hannah took immense interest in Swan's business and his interests. She learned the art of Photography, before dry plates, Kodak cameras making it easy. Between the years 1873 and 1880 five children were born. Hilda, Isabel, Kenneth, Percival, and Dorothy. They were raised with the others as one big happy family.

Holidays

In August 1876, Hannah Swan and the family went to Moss Hill, a farmhouse near to Carlisle for a holiday. In the fields grew wild roses and honeysuckle, ragged robin, and water forget-me-knots. Nearby was the river Eden. The area was full of history, Lanercost Priory where Edward I lay dying, raging at his inability to wage warfare against the Scots. Nearby is Naworth Castle where the name of *'Belted Will'* leads the memory of border warfare in Tudor times. Nearby Brampton, where Prince Charles received the keys of Carlisle from a kneeling deputation. About a mile away *'Capon tree'*, is where some of his defeated followers paid the ultimate penalty for their loyalty to the Jacobite cause. The gravestone of Margaret Tee's *'Dale of 'Mumps Ha', (the original of Meg Merrylees]* described by Scot in *'Guy Mannering'.*

The whole area teams with History and tradition. Prior to the mines and other industry John Wesley described the landscape of Tyneside as 'Paradise on Earth'. This is the area where Hannah took the children to holiday for some months. Summers were important to the Swans and they had holidays sometimes at Dunbar, and sometimes at Whitby, where Swan met James Russell Lowell the poet known for *'The Vision of Sir Launfal'.* One year they visited Bamburgh Castle, which they rented. It had amazing romantic associations from Saxon times to the Jacobite uprising of 1715 and it overlooked the *'Long Strand',* of Northumberland and the Farnes and Holy island with the memories of early saints. The Fortress had a reputed ghost in the night nursery and a witch, said to be a toad that sat at the bottom of the Castle wall. The Christmas holidays were usually spent at home but in 1900-1901 the family spent Christmas in Switzerland. They stayed at Caux, where Swan practiced the less physical activity of Curling and Lugeing

Incandescent Lamp

The work of both Edison and Swan was independent, although each knew what the other was researching. The principle of generating electricity was attempted on a large scale after 1849 and the benefits were not seen until 1862 with the Dungeness Lighthouse. The first Commercial Electro lighting plant was installed consisting of a Magneto-Electro machine of a primitive type and a 'Serrin arc light' after this there was immense activity in electrical Engineering.

Names such as Varley, Wheatstone, Siemens, Gramme, Bush, Wilde, and Homes. Dynamo Electric machines of various types were designed, more efficiently after 1877. At this point street lighting, lighthouses, and large buildings could be fitted with lighting economically. An invention of a Mercury Vacuum Pump by Herman Sprengel in 1865 made Swan rethink his incandescent lamp. One trouble was the rapid wearing and breaking of the carbon. The other was the obscuration of the lamp bulb by a black smoke. Swan got over this problem by passing a strong current through the filament so as to render it brilliantly incandescent, whilst the process of exhaustion was continued at high temperature. It was found possible to obtain a vacuum. It was further found that the carbon, because of being exhausted and sealed, did not waste away. This procedure in 1878 proved invaluable and solved the problem of lighting by incandescent lamp.

At a meeting in Newcastle Chemical Society, held on December 18th 1878 Swan was able to show an incandescent carbon lamp which consisted wholly of a glass bulb pierced with two Platinum wires supporting between them a thin straight carbon conductor 1/25 inch in diameter. On January 17th 1879, a lecture with the bulb was repeated and the Sunderland Echo of January 18th reported that the bulb was exhibited working. News quickly spread round Tyneside that Swan had solved the problem of the incandescent lamp by means of a vacuum lamp and Swan delivered his lecture and exhibited his lamp on February 3rd 1879 to seven hundred people of the Literary and Philosophical Society of Newcastle, Sir William Armstrong presided. A further lecture was given in front of five hundred at the Town Hall Gateshead on March 12th 1879, but the lamps were not patented until 1880 British Patent no. 8.

Thomas Alva Edison the young, now famous, American inventor was making similar experiments, in his well-equipped laboratory at Menlo Park, New Jersey, where he employed one hundred people. In October 1878 an announcement was made from America that caused a terrific slump in English gas shares, it was that Edison had solved the incandescent problem. The American Press was now making daily claims saying that he had done this by using carbonized paper. Swan had tried this theory previously without success, to this end he wrote to Edison informing him that this method was a failure. Edison had applied for a British Patent, even though he was aware that his lamp was not 100%. Swan was urged to register his, but knowing that he had exhibited his lamp working on two occasions did not rush to do this. Consequently on

November 10th 1879, Edison registered his, as a British Patent in broad terms as follows, *[A carbon filament within a* glass *receiver from which air had been exhausted]* This patent would have important effects on the business of both Edison and Swan in the future. Early in 1880 Edison discontinued the use of carbon paper adopting carbonized strips of Bamboo. It was observed that more than a year after Swan had invented and adopted parchmentised thread as a filament material; Edison was still using Bamboo.

London

Early in 1883, the Swan family moved south where they had a new home *'Lauriston'*, at Bromley a small Kentish town that had open surroundings. Lauriston stood on the extreme northwest fringe of the town, near to the old coaching road, which ran through Lewisham to London. The house was a newly built good-sized house with three acres of grounds where all kinds of trees grew. The gardens were re-designed by John Hancock in a simple natural way where the seasonal flowers were brilliant. In hard winters the tennis court was turned into a skating rink. The sheet ice being gradually sprayed and formed as they do in Switzerland. By this method a good surface was possible and the Swan children loved it. An arc light was rigged up and Swan, with his beard, looked like Father Christmas with his fur coat and he served coffee and soup to the skaters. Across the London Road opposite to *'Lauriston'*, stands the old college built by the Bishop of Rochester in the reign of Charles II. To the newcomers from the north they found great charm in the picturesque little town. Both children and plants seemed to thrive far better than they did at Low Fell for some reason, where living conditions were more rigorous.

Litigation

In 1885 litigation was started between Edison and Swan, with regard to the incandescent lamp. The evidence was laid before judicial consideration. Swan had already exhibited his lamp in December and many other occasions in 1879, before the date of Edison's British Patent in November 1879. Later as Swan and Edison merged, it gave them the valuable monopoly, as many other companies were waiting in the wings for developments, in fact even though Swan was accepted as the inventor of the incandescent lamp, the Edison Patent with the broad fundamental claims was valuable to them

Incandescent Lamp Manufacture

A small Company was formed in Newcastle *called 'The Swan Electric light Company Ltd';* a factory was also started at Benwell, Newcastle. A further Factory for the filaments and glass bulbs was opened at Birkenhead, Liverpool. The glass blowing was done here. No glass blowers could be found in England to carry out this task apart from Fred Topham from Birkenhead, and it was decided to engage German glass blowers to work under the supervision of Topham, who instructed them in this art, these German's came from the Thurlingian district of Germany.

The first residence apart, from his own, to be lighted by incandescent lighting was his friend Lord Armstrong's Cragside, near Rothbury. Swan personally supervised this instillation in December 1880. It was the first hydroelectric generating plant in the country. The motive power was supplied from the waterfall in the Cragside grounds. The success of this project started a chain of lighting events starting with Alnwick Castle, the Northumberland Home of Sir William Thompson, Sir William Spottiswood, president of the Royal Society. Shipping came next all of the giant liners requiring the lighting. After many mining explosions in the North of England Swan was approached on numerous occasions to see if he could help with the problem. To this end Swan produced a miners lamp with a firedamp indicator in 1886, and he visited Urpeth Busty Pit, near Birtley [sunk by William Coulson]. There were four in the party and Swan also used another electric lamp which he designed for underground conditions and it revolutionized mine work, the miners were amazed at the clarity of the lamps.

Honours

In October 1901, Durham University conferred upon him the Honorary Degree of MA; in 1902 the Royal Photographic Society awarded him the Progress Medal for the invention of the Autotype Process. The Medal of the Society of the Chemical Industry was given to him in 1903 for conspicuous service in Applied Chemistry. In December 1904 the Royal Society awarded him with the Hughes Medal for his invention of the Incandescent Lamp and other electrical inventions. The President, Sir William Huggins, when presenting the medal at the Royal Society mentioned his inventions in dry-plate photography, which increased the powers of experimental investigation. The Honour of Knighthood was awarded to him in November 1904.

These were the days when the Swans were living in London and where he was a Director of Public Companies, The Edison & Swan Electric Light Company, and the Notting-hill Electric Lighting Company. During his later years in London, Swan had financial anxiety, through having to pay large sums of money on behalf of a friend in his younger days. This person had been a financial backer when he needed investment cash early in his life and later he stood as guarantor to a bank for him. The amount Swan had to pay by far outweighed the initial amount after exorbitant bank interest. The sum was eventually met but not without pain, and it effected his personal family fortune, and taxed his strength and well-being and he was no longer up to the strain that life in London made upon his life and the time had now came to change his home. and to live in Surrey.

Warlingham

Swan's heart trouble and the stresses and strains of living in London brought him to Warlingham. This area gave him a quieter environment and in the autumn of 1908 they moved away from London to a house called 'Overhill', at Warlingham. A village on the north downs of Surrey. The fine air of this area and his undisturbed life made a marked beneficial improvement to his health and he was again able to further his experiments. During the summer of 1909 he was able to travel back to Newcastle to attend to important business, and he remarked as he headed North to 'God's Country'. Some of his observations as he headed north were, 'When we are abreast of the Cleveland Hills, past Thirsk wild roses were in abundance. Durham! Glorious in the mellow light of a far sunset, we go right on, without a moment's haste to drink the beauty of it. The most precious things are the most neglected! Ravensworth! Low Fell! The Tyne with its new bridge, which must not be crossed till after to-morrow when the King has proved that it, is safe for his subjects. The Old Castle and the new! A very good journey.

The End Of Swan's Mission

Swan was naturally endowed by nature with a good constitution and a virile physique. He had led a life of moderation calculated to preserve his life. Not a rigid tea-totaller, he seldom drank wine or spirits. He was a non-smoker, except on occasions to be sociable in company. Later in life symptoms of heart trouble affected him and he studied ways of prevention, this and good nursing, with the help of his nurse Miss Gosling, a trained nurse, and also his doctor, Dr. Etches, who attended him at Warlingham. In June 1913 he attended his sons wedding at London. This was on his 85th birthday, where he enjoyed the sight of all of his friends and relations.

The following year on May 26th 1914 Joseph Swan's health suffered a marked change. This particular May was rather cold. Doctor Sir Thomas Barlow was called on that day and he pronounced him to be very ill but in no immediate danger. The same night his heart failed and in the early hours of May 27th. 1914, he passed peacefully away. He was buried at Warlingham Church Yard. Carved on his tomb are the lines of Tennyson *'Day Dream'*, which was often on his lips.

"Were it not a pleasant thing
To fall asleep with all one's friends;
To Sleep thro' terms of mighty wars,
And wake on science grown no more,
On secrets of the brain, the stars,
As wild as ought of fairy,' lore."

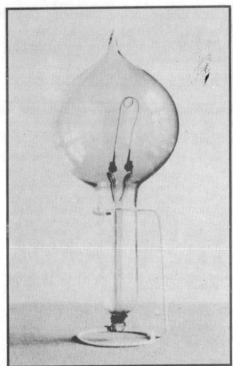

Above retail chemist advertising for Swan & Mawson
Left
Swan Incandescent Lamp; produced at Benwell, Newcastle uponTyne 1881. Below; Swan in his laboratory at Holland Park London:

Brilliant inventor
Sir Joseph Wilson Swan:

Cragside Northumberland; *the seat of Lord Armstrong, a great friend of Swan and where he exhibited his Incandescent light bulbs for the first time:*

JOSEPH WHITWORTH
(Brilliant Engineer)

J oseph Whitworth's early life may have given him the inspiration he needed to build the great engineering business that he did. This combined with the brilliant discoveries, which he made that revolutionized engineering principles along with armaments, and he was undoubtedly one of the greatest engineers that ever lived. Joseph was barely twelve when his father deserted him and the rest of the family to become Reverend Charles Whitworth. It was described by Whitworth later as utter selfishness, his father's decision to foster him and his brother out, but even worse to send their sister Sarah to a Bristol orphanage was a disgrace for a man of religion as he claimed he was.

These terrible acts by his father made Joseph, even at twelve, more determined than ever to succeed in life and also not have the slightest to do with his father. He carried this out for the remaining fifty-five years of his father's life.

Charles Whitworth and Sarah Hulse married when Charles was twenty-one and Sarah was twenty-three. They married at Stockport Parish Church on 14th. March 1803. The first child was Joseph born 20th December 1803. Their home was at the time a two bedroom dwelling house at the top of stone steps leading from a place called Fletcher's yard, later this house was renamed 13 John Street. Joseph was hardly fifteen months when Orchard Street Congregational Church accepted his father as a Sunday school class leader. It must have entered the mind of Charles Whitworth at this early stage of his life that a full time position could be an escape route from his fatherly responsibilities. The man most responsible, it could be argued for Charles Whitworth's journey into faith, was the Reverend William Evans. He was a charismatic preacher. From the start he had set out to find young men for his faith and to teach others. Whitworth was waiting to be found and was very attracted to Bill Evans like metal to a magnet.

Stockport, over the following twenty-five years, grew six times over to seventy thousand people by 1852. These were the days of the Catholic protest riots; there were regular mill fires and machines vandalized. In 1812 eight machine vandals were taken to Newcastle and executed. These were the dangerous times around Stockport and Manchester. Irish immigrants were taking all of the weaving jobs for less pay, and at the same time the Catholics had no voice in Parliament. These were the times of the Catholic Emancipation in England and they had to fight for their very existence in society. Joseph's father was a well-known reed maker and if the mob had smashed local looms, people like Whitworth were watched in case they repaired them. The Whitworth family was in constant danger of having their windows smashed or themselves assaulted.

Sarah Whitworth in March 1813 gave birth to a daughter whom her father baptized Sarah. The baby, though sickly *(after, mother and baby had serious complications after fever)* survived, but mother died early in the year of 1814 aged 34. The two boys grieved the loss of their mother tremendously, so much so that they suffered utter despair. Their father was at a loss what to do, his best friend the Reverend Bill Evans had died three years previously. Charles Whitworth took the extraordinary decision to point the family in four different directions, after deciding to take on a post as a full time Reverend. When the time came to say goodbye it would probably be the final time Joseph would ever see his father. Little Sarah went to an orphanage at Bristol where she stayed for ten years. The task of finding foster homes for the boys was hard. John went to live in Queensland, Australia where he married in 1830. Joseph was fostered by a middle class family but required his street-wise experience to survive. Joseph was so desperate to make something of his life, in the July 1820 the year following 'Peterloo', he ran away. He was not yet seventeen.

Manchester and Apprenticeship

Joseph added a year on to his age saying he was seventeen. The first company he went to for a job was 'W. J. Crighton & Company' who offered him a start. The factory had modern machinery and he stayed there fourteen months. From Crighton's he moved a short distance to 'Marsdon & Walker', of Water Street, well known for Textile Machinery. He again stayed there for the same length of time and interestingly, he thought more of his own skills than of the Company. He was already doing the work of a skilled tradesman and he would not be twenty-one, until Christmas 1824. He made a further move but this time as a skilled millwright working for 'Houldsworth & Company' who possessed an internationally renowned cotton mill in Lever Street. They paid him the full rate for the job. Later in life he said that it was the happiest day of his life, being paid as a journeyman. He left Manchester for London on his birthday December 1824. During these years Joseph's father having, got rid of his obligations, was allocated a small bursary and with it a place at the Congregational College, the Academy, at Idle near Bradford. The tutor was a brilliant classics scholar, the Reverend William Vint. The date was December 1824, & ten students were in residence.

Joseph was now heading for London, he was twenty-one years of age and it was Christmas, 1824. On his journey to London he travelled via the canal sleeping wherever he could. He managed to save a little for his journey out of his tradesman's wages. Joseph met a young lady on one of the barges and got a lift. She was twenty-four years of age and a bargeman's daughter from Tarvin, Cheshire, her name was Francis Ankers. It was love at first sight, and they eloped making their way towards Nottingham, having first of all called at Ilkeston to get a priest to marry them. On the 25th February 1825 Fanny Ankers bargee's daughter married Joseph Whitworth. Frances, not being able to read or write, marked the Register with a cross. The couple endured some very bumpy years together and she ended her days reasonably well off living near her sister's home in Cheshire. At the time of this strange marriage, neither Fanny's father nor her sisters ever thought that the marriage would survive thirty, mostly happy, years.

London

Joseph Whitworth commenced work at London in May 1825 at Maudsley as an ordinary bench fitter. Whitworth remained here for three and a half years. Maudsley at the time employed one hundred and twenty people and they were very impressed with the standard of Joseph's engineering skills. Maudsleys was the Company where household names such as Brunel, Nasmyth, William Muir and Bryan Donkin worked – after Whitworth had left. Whitworth remained in London for eight years. After Maudsley's he went to Holtzapffel then to 'Wright's & Sons' then 'Joseph Clements'. At each company learning new skills with machinery and general engineering skills. Maudsley had a similar start as Joseph, and was roughly the same age. Maudsley had such a name that the best engineers wanted to work for him. Unfortunately, he was destined to die a relatively young man. Maudsley for some time worked for Bramah where he made engineering history making a crude lathe and improving it by adding a slide rest, which was actually patented by Bramah. Maudsley asked for more money than his thirty shillings a week. Bramah refused so Maudsley left, setting up his own workshop.

This was terribly mean and shortsighted of Bramah, and these were the people, with whom Whitworth was competing in his early working life. Whitworth longed to go into business himself and he could see the potential of mass production, especially further north. The time he spent in London had been invaluable. He had made the best possible use of London libraries and learned societies and he was now prepared to put his knowledge to the test. He and his wife, Fanny, packed their bags and booked two outsider seats on the Manchester bound Lancashire Express Mail Coach. Both Fanny and Joseph had one thing in common; they lived for the future and hoped for better times, which they both knew would definitely come.

71

Back in Manchester 1832

Joseph was now twenty-nine and he was back in Manchester after some eight years, this time having his wife with him. It was the start of the cotton boom. Manchester was at this time growing into the engineering capital of the world. Joseph Whitworth, just prior to Christmas, began searching for suitable premises for a small workshop; he had little money and wanted one or two simple machines included in the premises. He found what he was looking for in Port Street. He took over the premises and proudly screwed his name above the door. Joseph Whitworth Toolmaker from London.

For some reason Whitworth could not get the business off the ground and he moved on. Joseph did not feel right at Port Street; even though he worked from dawn to dusk he lasted there only six months. He now searched for alternative premises and he found these in May 1833. He again screwed his name above the door at 44 Chorlton Street. Here he sensed he was going to have success. Either for his own use, or when selling machinery, he hated credit and this slowed down his early progress. He forbade machinery leaving the premises unless it was paid for in full. His wage bill from May to July 1833 was £2.10s a week, rising to £21 in October; by April 1834, it was £50 a week.

Manchester was also fast becoming a locomotive centre of importance, and for a short time equalled the North East of England for production. By now Whitworth was working closely with Nasmyth, who had opened a workshop close to his own, on his return to Manchester. Fairbairn got on very well with Whitworth but he distanced himself from Nasmyth for some reason. In 1847 Fairbairn's *'Thames'*, shipbuilding collapsed wreaking havoc everywhere. By this time Fairbairn was drained physically, financially, and mentally. His two sons proved not to be talented ship builders, much to the dismay of Fairbairn. John Scott Russell and I. K. Brunel used part of Fairbairn's yard to construct the famous Great Eastern. Whitworth talked openly of the need to standardize precise measurement. People said that it would require new machinery, improved skills, higher wages and it was generally thought that many small engineering shops would go bankrupt. It was at Maudsleys that Joseph first saw a bench micrometer in use. Maudsley claimed that his micrometer gave him absolute truth and he humorously called it his Lord Chancellor. Whitworth's early measuring techniques progressed during 1834-36 and it was then he built his first comparator. Knowing fully he would also need accurate length gauges, he set about designing these. His measuring system was fully in use at his own premises before the board of trade became interested in them. The simplicity of his system was easy to see, but manufacturing the apparatus took three hard long years. In later years people asked just how accurate was Whitworth's 1860 gauging; the answer was almost as good as that of 1910 precision grinding and lapping machines.

Each stage of development from templates to drawing practice slotted in to the working practice. The plane surfaces and measurement then the gauges. then finally the drawings to co-ordinate the whole thing. Towards the end of 1842 Whitworth was producing fifty tons of machinery a week and his employment went from 277 to 636 in 1851, this, in just over two and a half years. His output increased to over two hundred tons a week. It was during the early 1860s that Joseph had some contact with William Armstrong. For some time now Whitworth wanted to abolish the use of cast iron for making gun barrels. He wanted to introduce his own breech loading guns made from solid fluid compressed mild steel. After 1875 Bessemer and Siemans-Martin, methods would make Whitworth re-think the steel question.

On 11 June 1855, a Select Committee reported that Whitworth's evidence was so overwhelming that his standard yard measurement constructed, of the same length as that of the Royal Commission, be legalized as the secondary standard for comparisons with local standards of measure throughout the country, and that his standard *'Whitworth'* foot and inch have the same sanction attached to them. Whitworth became a member of the Small Arms Commission. He insisted on including in the Commission's report a proviso that all government contract work is checked against templates and gauges, and that each gauge should be numbered on each drawing. By 1856 his workforce went a little further when they worked to three-dimensional drawings (First Angle). They further checked each machined piece against Whitworth's 'Go, No-go' gauges.

Road Sweeping Machine

Like Fairbairn, Whitworth often walked to work in the early days, through the Manchester streets and was constantly appalled by the dirt that had built up in the streets and in 1847 he invented and produced a horse drawn road-Sweeper. He costed the invention against the hard labour of sweeping the streets. Whitworth attempted to apply mechanical aids to as many operations as possible thus attempting to raise the standard of living.

America

Following the British success with the 1851 British Great Exhibition, America decided to go ahead with an industrial exhibition in New York in May, 1853, eventually opening on 10th July, 1853. England wished to compare British Industrial Techniques against America. Two years previously Britain appeared by far in advance, especially in armaments. A trilogy of people was asked to attend the exhibition and report back to England they were: Joseph Whitworth, George Wallis and Professor John Wilson. George Wallis was headmaster of the school of Art, Birmingham, and he was also the head of the only school of rifle design in Britain.

The Commissioners left the Thames on the 10th May 1853, on the Steam Sloop *'The Basilisk'*, and the Frigate 'Leander' accompanied them across the Atlantic. They landed at New York two days late and obviously had a bad crossing. Earlier, Charles Dickens described a crossing to Boston he and his wife had made earlier:

'The noise, the smell, the closeness, was intolerable, the sea was stupendous wet, and the decks were rolling'.

Catherine, his wife, and the maid were constantly thrown about the decks. The 'SS *Britannia'*, was an unforgettable experience and Dickens never repeated the trip for twenty-five years. When he did the same trip in 1867 he said he was never sick and made after dinner speeches, had huge meals and thoroughly enjoyed the whole thing. Dickens description of his trip probably affected more British engineers going to the exhibition. The 'SS *Basilisk'*, docked at New York on 26th May. Whitworth and the others quickly went ashore and boarded a train to Washington D.C. On the way Wallis and Whitworth visited some factories at Philadelphia and Baltimore. Whitworth's observation of technology and ideas in repetitive production was far in advance of England, although England's tool making quality was by far in advance of America. The proportion of hand slide lathes was found to be far more in America than England and most had powered cross slides and most were suspiciously like Whitworth designs. The machine shops were tooled very much like Whitworth set out his own in England. As early as 1835 Whitworth was exporting lathes and other machines to Francis Lowell the largest textile manufacturer in the States. Whitworth also sold machines to companies in Massachusetts and Connecticut. The machines, which Whitworth saw, were the offspring of Whitworth's quick return lathes, worm driven machines, and all of the machines were in common use in factories visited. Whitworth was very confident of his own engineering skills yet he wondered just how long it would take America to overhaul the lead he himself had given England. Overtake they certainly would not only England but also the whole world. He applauded American management for running the industry as it should run. In a matter of seven years after the 1854 report the American Civil War took place in which Whitworth had an armament interest. After the civil war, roughly about 1868 the American tool industry started to gain the lead Whitworth predicted. A high proportion of machinery was geared to mass production. William Gladstone, on becoming Prime Minister in 1868, appointed Robert Lowe MP as Chancellor of the Exchequer (Viscount Sherbrooke) he was anti-American in all he said and did. He attacked Whitworth for his American ideas on mass production. Robert Lowe was a brilliant orator and filled the House whenever he spoke. He was against anything that Whitworth advocated and when Whitworth received the Albert Gold Medal following Faraday and Louis Napoleon, he had a platform to put forward his findings, but Whitworth ducked the issue allowing engineering in America to easily excel against the rest of the World. Whitworth's policies were based on the fact that everyone should pay tax according to their income. His creed was mass production this became his culture in everything, locomotives, carriages, windows, doors, even bricks. In April 1857 Whitworth was elected a fellow of the Royal Society.

Whitworth Rifle

When Whitworth left America after the exhibition in 1853, they showered him with awards. Crowning him as England's greatest mechanician and gun-maker. Others in America called him a humbug and self-seeking publicist. There was a noticeable difference of opinion and the answer was that the Whitworth guns defeated the inferior guns of the Government. The Generals, because of this, rebuked Whitworth mercilessly.

The Crimean challenge had created a demand for military and naval engineering. Whitworth came up with a hexagonal-bored weapon. The more Whitworth perfected his arms the more competitions he won and the more he was rebuked. The quotes at the time were: *'He ended by producing the very best weapons ever invented'*, Mr. James A. Turner MP. 25th June 1861 and *'Mr. Whitworth should proceed to apply to heavy ordnance the same system of rifling which he has proved so singularly in small arms'*, General George Hay to Field Marshall Lord Hardinge 16th March, 1856. By 1857, after two years experimenting, Whitworth went on to produce guns, which easily out performed all of the rest. His pay off was a savaging by the War Department and also from the other armament manufacturers. A select committee to examine why the British army had not been supplied with a more efficient weapon than the French designed Enfield-Minnie rifle debated a motion. A question was asked why Whitworth's rifle had been rejected. The MP. Mr. Hussey Vivian (Glamorgan) went on to say: Mr. Whitworth's rifle beat the best rifles in the French army by two and three to one. Whitworth had even received congratulations from Louis Napoleon, Emperor of France on April 23rd 1867. The Times reported that the Enfield rifle had been completely beaten by the Whitworth, in accuracy of fire, penetration, and range. Using only half a charge, 35 grams of powder, its lead alloy bullet penetrated through seven inches of elm at a reduced distance of twenty yards a steel bullet went through a wrought iron plate 0.6 inches in thickness. The war department representatives were amazed; it was the first time that a rifle bullet had gone through an iron plate. During the year 1860,

Whitworth constructed many field guns with steel barrels designed to act as both muzzle loading and breech loading. All were high quality weapons suitable for the total defence department including the navy. Although negotiable the price was higher than Armstrong. For a 4.5 bore 32 pounder the charge was £400, for a 5.5 70 pounder it was £700, for his new, very big gun, a 7 inch – 120 pounder, hexagonal barrel, it was £1350, and double the Armstrong equivalent at Elswick. General George Hay said in the Mechanics Magazine, May, 1860, that Whitworth had solved the problem that he undertook with the rifle, on how to project to the best advantage a given quantity of lead with a given quantity of gunpowder. There is no other gun in England that can do it as good as the Whitworth rifle. The magazine went further to say that at this point it has been proved there is no reason to carry on with the production of the Enfield, *'How wrong they were'*.

Whitworth became a little fretful because of his extreme activity. He became quarrelsome with friends and said he was not well. Doctors advised him to rest more but he took no notice. Fanny seemed to get the brunt of all of his troubles. They had now been married thirty-one years and for the last ten, Joseph had spent most of his time at work or travelling. They were now both lonely people, both looking for companionship. They lived at the Firs with its long drive and its fifty-two acre estate and farm. Fanny never enjoyed living in the house at all, in fact she never felt right in the house at all. Joseph and Fanny grew more and more apart. Regular invitations came to civil functions addressed to Mr. & Mrs. Whitworth but more and more Joseph went on his own. HRH Prince Albert sent out an invitation for Joseph and Fanny to join him and the Queen at Osborne House, Isle of Wight, from 16th December 1856. Albert wished to personally try Whitworth's rifle. On the day Whitworth attended on his own and it was known at this time that Fanny preferred to stay with her sister at Tarvi. These days Joseph often asked his friend, George Wallis, to stay with him. Fanny never experienced any financial problems at all and settled into her new home, Forest Hall, having a fair income from Whitworth. Mary Louisa Whitworth's second wife became Mistress of Stancliffe Hall in April 1871, the house where Whitworth moved from the Firs. This was a beautiful estate costing £33.850 in the Derbyshire countryside. At first, Stancliffe stood on a bare hillside without any attractions other than magnificent scenery and with the advantage of bracing atmosphere. He transformed this bleak house into one of the most beautiful landscaped garden estates in England. Shrubs were ingeniously planted for effect. The Chronicle newspaper described the result of his work   *"The main roads are bordered with wide shrubbery borders filled with a profusion of choice rhododendrons, azaleas and other flowering trees and shrubs, intermixed with spiry conifers, bronze retinas pores and elegant birches. The rocks themselves are light fawn verging into rich chestnut brown and are captured with pernettyas and vacciniums. Of the larger plants occupying pockets on the rocks are glorious masses of white and yellow blooms, gorgeous bushes of gorse, thickets of rhododendrons, dauphines and holly's, conifers are everywhere, mostly flame like or pyramidial in outline".*

Whitworth and his new wife, Mary, shared a common interest in educational issues. Later, Whitworth wished to hand over *'Stancliffe'*, as a retirement home for retired engineering professors. Mary was the daughter of Daniel Broad Hurst a previous Manchester City treasurer, and from the age of eighteen had rubbed shoulders with people like Fairbairn, Tootal, Bright, and Edward Walters. Mary Louisa remained unmarried for twenty-one years before finally marrying Whitworth, almost as though she was patiently waiting for him. The life style with Joseph suited her down to the ground. In later years Joseph Whitworth and his wife spent their days involved in the estates, the *'Firs'*, and *'Stancliffe'*, travelling a great deal abroad. When Whitworth reached seventy-three he appeared to relax more and enjoy Stancliffe. The celebrated Gardner Edward Mimer and the architect T. Roger Smith rebuilt Stancliffe in the years 1871-72. Whitworth was particularly interested in his stud farm and trotting ponies. He also collected many paintings, watercolours being his preference. He admired William Etty, (His favourite) also collections of Thomas Creswick landscapes of the Lake District, and also Derbyshire. Both Mary and Joseph sat for commissioned portraits.

Whitworth recognized his latest heart palpitations to be a warning and it was about this time that he started to attend the Saxon church of St. Helen, Dailey Dale. Unfortunately, he had a disagreement with the vicar about village education. The last twenty years of his life, Whitworth spent only a small part of his life in engineering. He became chairman of his company and J. Manny Gledhill was appointed managing director. Whitworth set out his articles of Association in 1874. These were amazing and are as follows: *The establishing, managing and assisting of schools, libraries, banks, dispensaries, infirmaries, provident societies and clubs for the benefit of persons employed by the company.*

By these Articles he wished to supply education for his employees and apprentices. He also wanted to supply the services of a works doctor and medical room. The Articles of Association were passed in the spring of 1874 when he employed 780 people. Whitworth Company was one of the first to issue shares. These were £25 and could be paid for, by payments from wages. If because, of sickness, workers were required to sell the shares, or if they were leaving, then the shares could be re-sold to the company plus interest, at the price they originally paid. It was generally thought that on the death of Whitworth and his wife the company would be gobbled up by William Armstrong of Elswick. They were exactly right, as on the death of Lady Whitworth in 1896 the firm became Sir. William G. Armstrong Whitworth and Company Limited. Sir Joseph Whitworth died Saturday evening 22nd January 1887 at the English Hotel, Monte Carlo. He was a great benefactor, perhaps Britain's greatest benefactor. In his will drawn up December, 1884, it was clearly indicated by Whitworth that he wished the bulk of his estate should provide an educational foundation capable of carrying forward eligible pupils (Male-Female), to become superior workmen or pupil teachers. At the time of his death, the amount left by Whitworth and his wife was £1.8 million Sterling, and estimated to be valued at £95 million at today's values and, taking into account the undervalues of the two estates, it exceeds Lord Nuffield's magnificent legacy.

Joseph Whitworth was buried at the Church Yard of Darley Dale, Derbyshire, near a great Yew Tree which some say is 1000 years old.

Whitworth Hotel with the institute on right at Darley Dale after opening in 1890; the object being to give his workers the chance of further education:

Joseph Whitworth

Whitworth's early home 62 Upper Brook Street, Manchester, in 1839

Whitworth 12 pounder ; Joseph Whitworth 3rd from right: Manchester Central Library

L.S LOWRY

(Famous Painter)

R ight from the start of his life Laurence Stephen Lowry was not wanted, his mother, Elizabeth, badly wanted a girl and his father wanted anything that his wife wanted. Lowry lived until he was eighty-eight, every year it was said in total rejection. His fame coming in the final twenty years of his life. Among the buyers of his paintings were: Royalty, the world's largest Art Galleries and famous collectors, who paid massive sums for his paintings. Fame also came from elsewhere; he was offered an order of the British Empire, a Knighthood, an order of the Companions of Honour. He was also made a Royal Academician, and invited to dine at Downing Street. The Hall'e Orchestra celebrated his birthday and later, after his death, a pop-song was recorded on his life, which went to No. 1 in the charts. Three Doctorates were presented from Universities and he was offered the freedom of Salford.

Lowry wasn't much bothered really, some honours he accepted, some he rejected. Lawrence strived in life to bring forward love from his mother, which she failed to give him from birth. His mother was born in March 1858 in Manchester to Ruthhetta and William Hobson. Ruth being raised in the Isle of Man. Elizabeth's father carried on the business of a Hatter and was fairly prosperous. His brothers and cousins carried on the same trade. The family rented a series of red brick houses in the Oldham Road area of Manchester. This was where the manpower of the prosperous factories lived during the Industrial Revolution. This was the time of thriving northern mills and also the area where Lawrence got his inspiration for the majority of his paintings. Children running barefoot, woman old and gray before their time. Fighting and brawling drunken men, and of course, pawnbrokers. This is also the area William Hobson chose to bring up his family. Hobson took his family to church every Sunday and as each was born he had them baptized at St. Paul's, New Cross. Edward George, Ruth (died in infancy), Elizabeth, Mary and finally, Willie, who shamed the family. Elizabeth being prone to Bronchitis and Lassitude and received special attention

79

from her father and mother, as they thought she would not survive. She went on to be very bright at school in everything that she did, even at the age of eight she was awarded a first prize for merit. Her father doted on her. He died when she was eleven; the trustee in his will was James Jackson. A draper from nearby Bradford Street, he also died, leaving George Anderson a boot and shoe manufacturer, to act as administrator. Ruth Hobson also died of consumption in 1879. William Hobson and his wife left an estate of £1,500 in trust until the boys were twenty-one, or the girls married. The family carried on the Hatters business with the profits equally divided between the rest of the family. Elizabeth carried this out to the letter; the shop was at 50 Oldham Road.

Elizabeth progressed well over these years, mainly in music, and was giving lessons and earning extra money, she studied further attending lectures, two of these were *'Characteristic sketches of Great Musicians'*, and, *'The History of Pianoforte playing'*, she also attended organ recitals and received advanced music lessons from Mr. R. Leicester. The Sunday school at Bennett Street was well attended, especially by Elizabeth; contact was made with such people as William Morris, George Bernard Shaw, and Kropoton the Russian who fled Russia to teach Botany and Biology in Manchester. These were the years when Mr. Ford Maddox Brown painted a series of mural paintings in the large room at Manchester Town Hall, to commemorate the history of Manchester. At this time Manchester was also the centre of musical England. Charles Halle arrived from Paris, forming the famous orchestra. Chopin performed in the Gentleman's Concert Hall where the Midlands Hotel now stands. Hans Richter, friend of Wagner, succeeded Halle. Adolph Brodsky the Great Russian violist was a professor at Manchester College of Music where Carl Fuchs taught the Cello. Richard Strauss also visited Manchester over this period.

Although Elizabeth was a very good musician unfortunately her career never really took off. Possibly the competition at the time was too strong. She did, however, become a well-known accompanist to the best voices of the day and a very patient teacher of music. Her bronchial attacks became more and more frequent and her Lassitude more pronounced. Elizabeth and Robert Lowry were married at St. Andrews. In Blackley, they had a short honeymoon in Lytham after which they set up home at 8 Barratt Street, Old Trafford.

Laurence Stephen Lowry was born November 1st 1887. Like the rest of the Lowry's he was prone to a weak chest resulting in coughs and colds in abundance. When his mother could even bear to look at him she thought that he was ugly, while his father adored him on sight. Lowry's own recollection of his youth was full of gloom saying he had no happy memories of his childhood, also saying he had a one track mind – 'poverty, and gloom, my early life was not nice at all, none of my pictures are happy! You will never see the sun in any of them'.

Lowry also said he never received any presents on his birthday neither at Christmas. It was noticeable that he owned many books that were inscribed with best wishes, and with Mother and Father's love. What is known is that his mother asked when he was born, "is it a girl" and when the answer was that it was a boy, she cried uncontrollably beyond reason. Later Lowry said that he was a horrible child and his father wanted to throw him out of the window because he would not stop crying when he was five months old. When asked about his father, Lowry said he just sat on the sideline, he never saw him very pleased neither did he see him very annoyed with anything. His father once spoke about his sister Mary, when she died he said, "I suppose I better go to the funeral", and he went on to say "you know it happens to all of us", he went on further saying "I don't see why I should go to the funeral", and he didn't. A story about young Lowry was told by Robert who tried to recruit him for a junior football game at St. Clements's, some said he found it hard to make friends and was a bit of a snob. Others later said they put him in goal and he threw himself all over the place, and there was mud all over him. The other team did not score at all and he was treated as a hero. He went home covered in mud and his mother nearly had a fit. They tried to get him to play again but he refused.

There was a further story about Lowry smoking when he was twenty-three he fell asleep with a cigarette burning in his hand and nearly set fire to his bed, Lowry never smoked again. The year was 1903 and Lowry was now fifteen and it was debated just what direction in life he should take. Sometimes his father took him to the Art gallery, but at the time he wasn't very interested, at home the only picture they had was an oleograph portrait of Beethoven. It had been noted that Lowry drew and doodled a great deal. He went to art school where he begged to enrol. He started in the freehand drawing class, moving on to other classes as time moved on. When they thought he was sufficiently advanced, they put him in the life class where he practiced life drawings for twelve years. Lowry thought that this was a good foundation for painting.

There was a problem teaching painting, as everyone's colour sense is different. With drawing it is totally different you either get it right or wrong, according to what the drawing subject is. Robert Lowry's employer Jacob Earnshaw died on October 1908, and Robert sat back waiting for promotion and the partnership that he was promised years before. It never came, and all of the years of loyal service seemed to have gone down the drain. John Earnshaw's son and junior partner never offered Robert anything. *(John Earnshaw had a remarkable resemblance to Lowry's 'The Manchester Man'.* With the realization that he would not get the promotion, a deep sense of disappointment came over Robert – he never recovered. His eyes drooped and his moustache also. These

81

characteristics were noticeable in photographs, rather than Lowry's painting of him.

By 1909 Robert accepted that the family must make strict economies, they moved to 117 Station Road, a four-bedroom house with an annual rent of £26, basically they had moved to the other side of town. Lowry had found another job over this period, as a claims clerk for 'General Accident Fire & Theft Insurance Corporation'. He was now twenty and his annual salary was £46.16s. A high percentage of which went to pay for pencils, paints, brushes, paper – and fees for his art classes.

It was in 1912 that Lowry completed a pastel called, *'Mill Worker'*, he also completed two oils of *'Morning'* and *'Evening'* views looking south to Pendlebury from Clifton Junction. There was also a view of factory chimneys with no figures in them. Lowry's father was burdened with debt at this time. Robert tried everything to preserve the status quo. He borrowed from friends and family, life insurance policies, moneylenders. This was the time of the great slump in England and also the time of the Great War. It seemed to have passed Lowry by. When asked why he did not go to war he would say, *'they would not have me'*, when he was questioned further he said he was declared unfit for active service. After a medical on April 10th 1916, at Bury Barracks he was classed as grade 3B and exempted from all duties except Garrison Duty. Lowry's problem was flat feet.

From his early College days Lowry enjoyed a close friendship with George Parker Fletcher, at the time he was a bachelor. Like Lowry, he was devoted to music and the arts, also the theatre and hiking. George soon married and Lowry made friends with his brother, Frank Joplin Fletcher, who was a photographer and studied the craft at Manchester School of Art. He was roughly the same age as Lowry and had similar tastes. They were soon visiting musical events together, Halle at the Free Trade Hall and Grieg's Posthumous Quartet. They went to see Horniman's Repertory Company and the young Sybil Thorndike in *'Hindle Wakes'*. Lowry had completed a portrait of Frank Joplin Fletcher and it remained behind the wardrobe until after his death in 1955, when his son, Philip, presented it to Salford City Art Gallery. Lowry failed to respond to Frank's death and did not attend the funeral or even send flowers. He did the same when his brother George died. He was in an advanced state of senility, when George was aged ninety-one in 1967. Phillip Fletcher was hurt tremendously by Lowry's lack of sympathy for his friends.

Lowry was now thirty-one years of age and up until then had not exhibited one painting. Now, as a member of the academy, he submitted three works for inclusion in the annual exhibition at Manchester City Art Gallery. In February the exhibition took place and Lowry's pictures were accepted. They were *'Portrait of an Old Woman'*, 15 guineas *'Landscape'*, at six guineas, *'Pencil Drawing'*, four guineas. Although Lowry did get a mention from the Manchester News reviewer, he did not make a sale. The *'Portrait of an old Woman'*, now hangs on the same gallery walls on permanent loan and it was insured in 1959 for £7,500. Not only did contemporaries rubbish Lowry's work, they sneered and laughed out loud. One of those that laughed loudest was Mr. Maxwell Reekie *(later vice president of the academy)*, a rather large Scotsman who painted Scottish Castles and also James Chettle, who had rather large ears and painted water colours, and who later Lowry spoke well of. Chettle talked about Lowry's funny cat in one of his paintings, Lowry said it wasn't a cat it was a dog.

After the 1919 Manchester City Art exhibition Lowry never even bothered to exhibit any more work for two years. He drew *a Woman in a Hat'* giving it to Master Percy Warburton who he later befriended. Lowry completed one or two street scenes over this period and he took them to the 'Manchester Guardian' critic for his opinion. Taylor said, "This will never do, you'll have to do better than that, can't you paint the figures on a light background? "How do I do that," said Lowry "It's for you to find out", was Taylor's reply. Lowry was mad and he went home and completed two pictures on chalky white background. "That will teach him," said Lowry. He showed Taylor these pictures "That's right," said Taylor.

This is the technique that Lowry followed throughout his life. The figures had to stand out from an almost chalky white background. It was possible to drop the white a little but it can't be lifted up. In 1924 Lowry made an experiment, which fascinated his father. Painting a piece of wood flake white six times and allowing it to dry. It was left six or seven years after being sealed. At the end of that time the same procedure was followed and the newly painted wood was lily white the other being a beautiful creamy, gray-white. The point he was making was that the best of his paintings would be available when he was dead.

Lowry observed the painting by William Strang over this period. It was extremely chalky and he wondered how it was possible to exhibit it at this time. Lowry saw the same painting at the Walker Art Gallery in Liverpool and it was gorgeous. The white had changed to a beautiful colour of creamy white. The exhibition continued for two weeks and Lowry never sold a painting. The oils were priced at £25, the smallest was £5. In 1921 most were not available under £1,500 *'The Lodging House'*, a strong pastel listed at ten guineas was bequeathed to Salford City Art Gallery, where it hangs in the permanent collection and is insured for £1,500. A flake white print called *'Sudden illness'*, was sold by the artist to the collector Monty Bloom in the fifty's for £4,000, but in a further two days he bought it back for £6,000. *'Hawkers Cart'*, is in the Royal Scottish

Academy, at Edinburgh, and *'Pit Disaster'*, went to Geoffrey Bennett in Carlisle; *'A Doctors Waiting Room'*, *was* bought by Salford in 1959 original price ten guineas now priced at £7,000; *'Coming out of School'*, was bought by Duveen Fund, for the Tate Gallery.

Lowry's father was more aware of his son's early success than his mother, and it brought him much pride and joy, Robert kept reviews of his son's achievements from newspapers. It was Lowry's father that got him to make one of his best drawings which was of Saint Simons Church. Robert told his son that it was due to be demolished. Elizabeth's attitude to her sons painting was rather curious and she rated his industrial scenes as quite without merit. Lowry received a letter asking him if he could write art criticism for a newspaper. When he showed his mother she laughed uncontrollably. When he actually did sell anything his father remarked, "this can't go on, it will go to his head." His mother was always rather bewildered. Lowry's happy days ended when his father died in 1932 this were also the year that he was first accepted by the Royal Academy. On Wednesday, February10th 1932, Robert Stephen Lowry died of pneumonia with his son present at, 117 Station Road, Pendlebury, aged seventy-four. Robert had a heavy cold over Christmas and Lowry saw him get progressively worse, even so, he struggled to complete his rent collecting. Lowry's mother, now seventy-three, took to her sick bed and stayed for seven and a half years relying solely on her son to care for her, which brought him to a state of derangement. Lowry sketched a simple cross for the stonemason in granite, this marks Robert's grave in Southern Cemetery in south Manchester, where all of the family are now buried.

Debts

When Robert died there were a few unpaid debts, £41 outstanding to the Wards, £50 owing to young Willy, £250 owed to John Earnshaw. The rent was outstanding, along with the gas bill, and a small overdraft at the bank. The Earnshaw debt was owed because Robert was not able to work and after Robert died Earnshaw approached Lowry for payment. Robert left his wife a total of £534.4.5d mainly insurance policies from which he had heavily borrowed. Furniture was valued at £25 and he had £1.2.5d in his pocket, his house was rented.

Elizabeth knew nothing of Roberts's debts even to his young nephew, Willie Hobson, the son of her elder brother Edward. Lowry thought it a disgrace and never spoke of his father's debts. Roberts's problems started in 1923. Willy was then working as a window cleaner in north Manchester. Willy readily loaned Robert money and so as not to overburden him he offered the money on a low percentage and the outstanding amount could be paid either monthly or quarterly. By 1925 Willy became concerned and he wrote to Robert saying that £50 was a lot of money to a window cleaner who works hard for every penny. Willy did not raise the matter again and when Robert died he said of him that he was brave good and kind man.

By April, Lowry had paid off all of the debts. In 1934 Lowry was elected as a member of the Royal Society of British Artists after exhibiting with them in 1933. His work was now travelling throughout England. *'A Hawkers Cart'*, was at Rochdale, in 1931, *'Going Home from the Mill'*, by invitation to Southport, 1932, *'The Lodging House'*, and *'A Football Match'*, to Bradford 1933, Oldham in 1936. Six Lowry's were included in a mixed exhibition. The same year two of his works *'Street Singers'*, and *'In Salford'* were selected from the Royal Academy and other London exhibitions for a show at Huddersfield Art Gallery; three more *'The Playground' 'Brokers Shop'*, and *'Market Square'*, were shown in the spring Exhibitions of works by Lancashire Artists at the Harris Museum and Art gallery, Preston.

The fact that Lowry could now put RBA. After his name did not increase his selling price. The year was 1937 and Lowry was now approaching his fiftieth Birthday. He was grateful for a sale every now and then although he had yet to show a financial profit against the rising cost of materials, frames and travel. Lowry painted solely to attempt to change his mother's opinion of him. He was raised in the belief that his mother had an instinctive eye for beauty and he acknowledged that judgment. If she saw only ugliness in what he achieved then it must be so, in spite of what others said, and only her changing her opinion of his work would make it any better. On October 12th 1939, his mother died unhappy to the end, she was eighty-three years of age. According to people closely associated with her she died as she lived, a spoilt stubborn, petulant woman who even in death refused to recognize what others freely acknowledged that her son was a great artist and had brought honour to her name.

Lowry shut off her bedroom keeping it only in his memories. There was no consolation for him as his fame came too late in life to change the opinion that his mother had for his work. Lowry was still a bachelor at fifty-two, he lived alone in the old house. He found it easy to show kindness, rather than to receive it. He made friends with a family living near to him the Leatherbarrows. Lowry asked if he could take their thirteen-year daughter to the pantomime and they readily agreed. Lowry took Kathleen to the Palace Theatre, Manchester early in 1940. The friendship with Kathleen lasted until she married in 1948. Later he had a photograph of her on his piano in a Wren's uniform. He also painted a portrait of her in uniform and refused all offers for it. Later when Kathleen was asked about the relationship she said that it seemed that he was enjoying the youth in her, and what he himself missed out of earlier in his life. The pantomime became a yearly occasion, right until Kathleen joined the Wrens at eighteen. Margery

Thompson was another young lady who used to accompany Lowry, and Kathleen to the Theatre. She said that he used to enjoy the occasion tremendously, so much so that on one occasion he opened the taxi door too soon and hit a lamppost. After the show the girls were taken for tea to the Squirrels Restaurant in Oxford Street, 'this is where the waiter drew the chairs out for us to sit on them', said Margery. The date was November 1st 1957 and it was Lowry's seventieth birthday. This day a photograph of Lowry and also a portrait of a young woman appeared in the Manchester Guardian. The portrait of the girl who was dark and slim with her hair parted at the centre and drawn behind her ears. This he said was his first portrait for over thirty years. He named it the *'Portrait of Ann'*, the newspaper reporter was curious, Lowry said she was twenty-five years of age, but not much more.

The portrait was a surprise for the Royal Academy, as everybody knew Lowry for his landscapes. For the first time Lowry was experiencing people asking about the sitter not unlike *'The Mona Lisa'*. Lowry said that she was his godchild Ann Hilder; people enquired about the young girl with the long black plait who's painting hung above Lowry's piano in the front room. He said that she was a friend of his from Lytham St Anne's. She died when she was still a girl and Lowry cried when talking about her.

The removal from Station Road came at long last. This was a dark house full of memories, with his mother's room still locked since she had died. After Robert had died, Louis Duffy acquired the property and carried on a strange relationship with his tenants. Sometimes his wife visited Elizabeth and was sometimes given a parting gift of one of Lowry's paintings. "Is it any good," her husband would say, "I'll give you a bob for it. Lowry always used to say that all of his paintings were good. Duffy began to get complaints from other neighbours about the overgrown garden and dirty windows and eventually Duffy advised Lowry to swap houses with himself, one reason being he had seen two deaths in the house and he also needed a much smaller house. A further reason being that Duffy's family was growing up and needed more space.

In a short while, Lowry commenced his life at 72 Chorley Road. He never really settled here and later friends advised him that a house had become vacant at a village called Mottram-in-Longandale on the fringe of the Derbyshire peaks, and this is where Lowry made his new home. Almost at once he started painting, one painting in particular was *'Laying a Foundation Stone'*, which Salford City people said was an insult to Lancashire. Lowry enjoyed telling the story and it was he that was invited to complete a painting about the occasion and attend the foundation Ceremony. When he got there, there were four rows of kids looking at a picture of pure misery, they were all singing a song that did not match the picture. The vicar looked ill and gazed in bewilderment as if he wished

86

he were elsewhere and the Mayor weighed down by his chain and wishing in his importance that it were all over. Lowry said that he had to leave, so as to have a good Laugh. A person kept bringing him back into the room in case he missed the big occasion of the unveiling of the foundation stone, for the new school at Clifton.

Lowry completed his picture and showed it to the Mayor who should have been most annoyed but he liked it very much. The City Fathers were very annoyed – and showed it. Things were made worse when Manchester City bought the painting. The Vicar, Canon Fletcher, was irate, telling Lowry that he was no gentleman, making fun of us like this. Lowry replied that he was entitled to paint what he saw. Lowry was accused of exaggerating the size of people's feet; Lowry replied that everybody seems to have big feet. One year later a picture appeared in a shop window off St. Anne's Square, it was of a dog with five legs, "Well I never", said Lowry, "I checked it very carefully before I let it go, it must have had five legs, because I only paint what I see. About this time Lowry retired from his job as a Cashier Book-keeper, at Pall Mall, he had a yearly pension of £200. The Chairman of the Company asked him if he would award the pension to another member of the company who had fallen on bad times, and Lowry readily agreed. His work was now exhibited world-wide, even Japan, and at the Museum of Modern Art in New York in 1959, the Robert Osborne Gallery in New York, and later in the same Gallery it was billed as 'The Englishness of English Painting', when a number of his paintings were exhibited.

Lowry had rejected many honours offered to him in his later years, they were forthcoming from Harold Macmillan, and in 1955 he was offered an OBE in the Queens Birthday list. A similar one came from Harold Wilson who proposed a CBE in 1960. Again in 1967 Wilson approached him this time offering a Knighthood. These he politely declined. Lowry said that all of his life he had been opposed to Social Distinctions of any kind consequently he said, regretfully, he must graciously decline the honours. A year later Edward Heath wrote to him tactfully asking him if he would be made a 'Companion of Honour'. Lowry replied, hoping not to give offence, saying that he had at all times tried to paint to the best of his ability and he said he hoped he would be always remembered for this work, rather than on the decoration that he had collected on the journey. Lowry turned down an offer by Harold Wilson to dine at 10 Downing Street; Wilson seemed to be slow in getting the message regarding his principles because he again contacted him. Lowry said that he wished to live the remainder of his life in peace free from publicity, which these honours would undoubtedly bring. He continued to repulse the belated attention from the establishment that he was now receiving. Lowry was attracted to many young ladies over the latter part of his life and one young lady was Carol Ann Lowry

L.S. Lowry.

(No relation to Lowry), she was the only child of William and Mattie who were born in Rochdale. The marriage ended and Mattie lived on her own with her daughter Carol. For years Mattie worked to give Carol a good education sending her to private schools. Carol was very artistic and Harold Hemingway advised Mattie to write to Lowry – him having the same name. Months later Lowry called unexpected at their home and so started a long friendship. Lowry paid her fees at the convent and helped with the rent and also arranged for Saturday morning classes at Rochdale College of Art where his friend, Leo. Solomon, was principal. Later Carol Ann was left the majority of Lowry's estate. Lowry had painted Mill scenes for thirty years and now it seemed that no one wanted them anymore. When having a one man show in London on October 11th 1961, it was headlined in the Daily Herald that hoards of cheque wielding admirers of the artist were trying to buy one of his paintings obviously on hearing that he was about to retire, mistaking this for his alleged change of direction in his style. Experts said that this kind of thing only happened when an artist died, all he had done was change direction, accepting that he had exploited industrial scenes for long enough.

It seemed a lifetime since his one-man exhibition, forty years ago at Mosley Street, when he did not sell one picture, now within an hour of opening more than a dozen pictures had been sold for over £1000. By 1956 McNeil Reid was pleading for his pictures, saying to Lowry, "I don't suppose you have a tiny industrial painting lying about. Lowry confided to Frank Mullineux saying, "the industrial scenes passed out of his mind, I could do it now, but I have no desire to." When appearing on Tyne Tees Television later, he elaborated on the same theme only adding sincerity saying the emotion would show in the picture. Each painting he did had a story to tell, *'The Man Drinking water'*, *'Man fallen down a Hole'*, *'Lady in a straw hat without a dog'*, *'The Business Man lying full stretch on a bench'* in the National Gallery. Lowry put his initials on his briefcase also putting initials on his own coffin on his *'Funeral Party'*, *'the Woman with the beard'*, *'The Working Mans Mona Lisa'* seen on a train from Cardiff to Paddington she had quite a nice face and a big beard. Lowry announced his retirement from painting soon after his eightieth birthday. He wasn't so much laying down his brushes as retreating from the world he found himself in. Lowry was tired, tired of work from which there was now no release from the meaningless fame. Now, all he wished was peace to pass his remaining years with his friends. Even in retirement Lowry was making vast sums of money. In 1972 his painting earned him £65,000 giving him a net total of £50,000. For all of this his lifestyle remained modest. For the year his sundry expenses amounted to only £47. The £15,000 difference between gross and net being for accountancy

88

and agent's fees. His light bill was only £69, he did not drink or smoke, he had three suits, one being spattered with paint.

Once in the Ritz Hotel in London he went for dinner and had an overwhelming desire to order egg and chips, especially when being served by a superior waiter. He kept his house temperatures sub zero, saying he never felt the cold. Later he made this into a game when art dealers came from the south into his sitting room, which was freezing, forgetting to put the electric fire on, then watching their expression and how long it took for their noses to turn blue or teeth to chatter, using it has a yard stick of their greed, the length of time before they complained of the cold.

One extravagance he did have was his use of taxis, even using the service to travel as far as Sunderland. Taxi drivers used to barter for his business as much for his interesting conversation than the money. As the years passed on Lowry became more and more mischievous. Once when he was travelling from Newcastle via Middlesborough, with Mickey Marshall, he stopped for lunch at the 'Wilson's Arms' a public house at Middlesborough. Lowry started a conversation with a little glint in his eye "Do you think it matters?" Lowry inquired. "No," said Marshall quick to catch the artist's train of thought. "I don't think they'll ever find out." After their meal they went for coffee in the lounge, which was very much like a railway carriage. On the wall was a moderate watercolour of the Hotel painted by a schoolteacher in 1923. At this point the room was now full. They all sat looking at the picture, "Do you think they know what they have got?" "Shouldn't think so," replied Marshall, "they wouldn't have it up there if they knew, it's an early one isn't it sir?" he went on.

By now everyone was looking at the picture, "it must be worth a few bob". Just then a man left the room and was later seen leaving with a painting under his arm. Sir John Bateman wrote a letter to the Guardian in 1975 saying, 'I would like to mention a Manchester subject he is L.S. Lowry, he is eighty, unmarried with no heirs; his paintings are so good that a permanent exhibition should be made, like 'Van Gogh' in Amsterdam or the 'Rodin Museum' in Paris'. The following morning the *'Manchester Guardian'*, said most British painters have to wait until they are dead before this kind of thing happens. L.S. Lowry is luckier than most it was said. Lowry laughed out loudly on reading the report, but for years it was seriously considered.

Lowry was not frightened to die, in some cases as you get older it is to be desired, the manner of the passing concerned him, he was known to say, "a married man lives like a dog and dies like a king. A bachelor lives like a king and dies like a dog. He had seen friends and family lose their fights for life. The Fletcher brothers, Frank and George, his mother and father who he missed tremendously right through his life. Now it was Lowry's turn. In the early hours of Monday, February 23rd 1976 nine days after his admittance into Hospital, Lawrence Stephen Lowry died in his sleep of pneumonia following a stroke. He had been a burden to no one; he lived as he died with humour dignity and courage. The funeral was held Friday 27th February 1979. The press was there, in scores, artists, dealers, collectors, and friends in fact anyone who wondered about this strange and great painter. The Reverend Geoffrey Bennett read the 23rd Psalm. Also thanking God for his life, work, and friends. It was a gray dismal day in Southern Cemetery, Manchester where Lowry was laid to rest in the same plot as his father and mother.

Lowry's Estate:

Here was a little intrigue after Lowry's death on just where the majority of his estate would go. He left a small Rossetti to his faithful friend and solicitor Alfred Hulme. £1000 to Bessie Swindles, four paintings as promised to Salford, and an inlaid Tompion Grandfather clock *(turned out to be a partial fake)* to Geoffrey Bennett. To Carol Ann he left his prize possession *'Prosperpine'*, plus the remainder of the estate valued at £298,459. Of his godchild Ann there was no mention. The price of the pictures soared after his death; he painted between 800 & 900 oils and also 3,000 drawings. By the first anniversary of his death his prices stabilized, by the second the prices had held. His constant question, "Will I live?" – he said it would take a hundred years. His paintings survive his detractors and his genius outlives all of his critics.

Lowry's *Mother and Father :*

*Below Lowry painted his own funeral; above this was the real thing on Friday 27th.
February 1979:*

Lowry's Cripples & 'Man lying on a Wall'

The Cripples(1949) Lowry said he operated on a gentleman in the distance and gave him a wooden leg (Salford City Art Gallery)

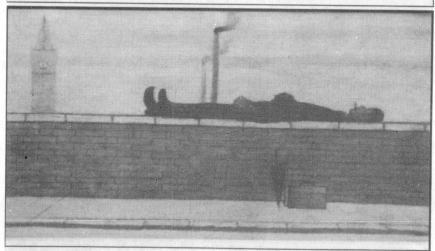

Man Lying on a Wall (1957) Lowry said he saw this sight ; he added his own initials (Salford City Art Gallery:)

GEORGE HUDSON
Railway King

The date was December 30th 1833, a group of tradesmen met in a hotel in York. Of the group three were Solicitors, several owners of small businesses, and also a number of small shopkeepers. The present Sheriff of York was also present, he was a coal merchant called Meek and he chaired the meeting. Recently the Liverpool to Manchester Railway had been shown to be a complete success and now South Yorkshire coal owners had came together to discuss building a line from Leeds to Selby, with options of proceeding further to Hull. It was hoped that in a short time South Yorkshire coal could be transported cheaply and swiftly to the vast Southern England market. This was the beginning of George Hudson's amazing journey to develop the Railway in the North of England.

George Hudson was a linen draper of College Street, York. His beginnings were rather obscure but by his own exertions he became a millionaire. He provided the whole of the north of England with railways which were built quickly and effectively using careful planning and supplying work for thousands of men. His friends, as well as himself became very rich. Later he fell foul of fraud by the methods used by him to create the finance for his projects. All of the Railways he created succeeded; because of this Hudson became known as the 'Railway King'. He was the son of a prosperous Yeoman farmer from the tiny village of Derwant between York and Malton. George was his fifth son being born in 1800. His father rather ignored education for him, thinking that he would make a farmer, but when George was nine his father tragically died leaving him to make his way the best he could.

George left school at fifteen, and it was at this time that he joined the business of William Bell as a bound apprentice in a linen shop, in College Street, York. George married a solicitor's daughter in 1821, Elizabeth Nicholson, on occasions she worked in the shop, and after the wedding the couple lived on the premises. Later, William Bell retired re-naming the business Nicholson and

Hudson. Later in his life, Hudson said that these days at the shop were the happiest of his life turning over £3,000 annually, 25% of which being profit.

In 1827 something happened which would change Hudson's total way of life pointing him to extreme financial heights and eventual ruin. A wealthy great uncle named Matthew Bottrill died aged seventy, leaving most of his fortune to George Hudson. The amount was a fortune of £30,000. Bottrill made the will on his deathbed when Hudson had been assiduous in attendance of the old man in his final hours. However the will was not contested and he became one of the richest men in York. In retrospect he said later that acquiring this money was the worst thing that could of happened to him as it led him towards the railways and eventual ruin.

The shop gradually disappeared into the background and Hudson progressed into higher society as part of the Conservative movement in the Country. Cholera was a problem in and around York at this time and Hudson served on the local Health Board where he made a name for himself. During the autumn of 1832 he stood for election at the local Tory council elections; progressing from organizer to treasurer of the party. Hudson became interested in banking and he formed the 'York Union Banking Company', which began trading in 1833 with a capital of half a million. Deposits were forthcoming from Sir John Lowther and other wealthy men and they began trading with London Bank 'Glyns', who's Chairman was also Chairman and chief promoter of the London Birmingham Railway and other lines. Hudson's bank would soon play a major role in the finance of other Railway Companies. At the meeting at 'Tomlinson's Hotel' at the end of 1833 Hudson became treasurer of the Railway Committee. He took up most of the shares offered for the York Leeds Railway and secured a famous engineer, Rennie, to survey the line – and this report was ready for the Committee in early 1834. Rennie actually proposed, on the grounds of economy, the use of horses.

Hudson visited Whitby later that year where he met George Stephenson. By this time Stephenson had been successful in designing two Railways which were both doing well. Stephenson and Hudson struck up a very formidable friendship, which lasted throughout both men's lives. There was a lull in the progress of the Railways in the North and Hudson took the opportunity to advance his political career. In 1834 the first reformed Parliament was dissolved and there was a General Election. With help from financial deposits from Sir John Lowther in the York Union Bank and also supported by James Richardson, acting as Tory agent, Hudson supported John Henry Lowther for one of the York seats in the election, £2000 being spent on the Poll and a further £1000 to reward, 'those that voted Tory'. The seat was secured and later there were objections against bribery used by the Tory's in securing the seat. In August 1835, Hudson and over sixty prominent citizens were summoned to London to testify before a Commons Committee on Election Petitions. Hudson, as party treasurer was cross-examined for two whole days and made to make a number of damaging admissions, the Tory's had been guilty of gross bribery. Hudson, although guilty of impropriety with funds for the good of the party, was welcomed home a hero and a true blue.

During the autumn of 1835 there was a public meeting with a deputation from Doncaster headed by its richest citizen, Edmund Becket Denison, to beg Hudson to arrange a railway to Doncaster. Hudson decided to be guided by Stephenson who advised the use of engines as opposed to horses, and Rennie's recommendation. Stephenson made his plans and now he informed the Committee of his proposals. His plan was to put in two railways right through the midlands, one from Derby by the hilly country to Leeds to be called 'The North Midland', and one from Rugby to Derby called 'The Midlands County Railway'. He had secured the Derbyshire and Notts. Coal owners and also a group of capitalists from Liverpool so success was guaranteed. Communication was then promised from Leeds to London. Hudson went quickly to Stephenson begging him to make the terminus of the North Midland line at York and not at Leeds. *'Mak all T'railways cum T' York',* he pleaded. Stephenson, thinking of fixed gradients on his lines, refused to change his original plans. Hudson thought up a clever deviation of his original plan that the York line should connect with Stephenson's line at Normanton. This was common sense approach, and they could also enlist Stephenson as their engineer, using his prestige for raising the capital.

The plan quickly took shape and the new line was called 'North Midland Railway', Hudson's strategy proved sound in that a group of Quakers who were originally involved in the 'S & D Railway' had proposed a line from Newcastle to York to be called the 'Great North of England Railway', and the two groups agreed to collaborate. Hudson wholeheartedly took the lead and the Committee was transformed into the 'North Midland Railway Company', with Hudson being its treasurer, James Richardson its Solicitor and one of Stephenson's assistants its Engineer. A survey of the line was carried out and the bill drafted for introduction to Parliament. Capital was then fixed at £300,000, which had to be raised. There was a lack of York investors but a group of London Capitalists added their weight and by 1836 the £50 shares began to sell. The York MP's including Lowther ensured an easy passage for the Bill through Parliament. By August the new committee was able to hold its first formal meeting and register the shares and also elect a board of directors. Sir John Simpson the Lord Mayor topped the poll, second, beaten by a single vote was Hudson. James Richardson, Alderman Meek Robert Davies *(Town Clerk)* and Richard Nicholson *(Hudson's brother in law)* were all elected. Later Hudson was chosen as their Chairman and his friend George Baker Secretary.

It was early in September that Stephenson staked out the first few miles of the line saying that it would be completed in eighteen months. They were over optimistic, Hudson in order to progress the bill through the House of Lords, had made an offer to Lord Howden *(He owned some of the land en-route).* Later Hudson attempted to get out of the deal but after litigation, Howden was paid £5000 by the Committee. Hudson had allowed him to be overreached and never forgot his lesson. In April 1837 Hudson commenced the contractors on the line, which was due to run from York across the Leeds-Selby line at South Milford at Altofts. The contractors imported their Irish navies and the companies stock rose together with Hudson's prestige in York. Stephenson had promised that the line would be the cheapest constructed, he actually invested £20,000 of his own money in the railway shares, and he had encouraged his friends to do the same. The Quakers were a little suspicious of Hudson, but they still invested their money on the venture, mainly due to their confidence in Stephenson. York City Council gave permission for a tunnel under the city with space for a station.

In April 1839 the first engine arrived from Stephenson's factory in Newcastle when it was christened the 'Lowther'. It was decided to have the opening ceremony on May 29th, when all of York celebrated the occasion. The Cathedral bells rang and everywhere in York there was signs of holiday and merrymaking. A large crowd of distinguished guests consumed early morning breakfast then, after a short speech by Hudson, four hundred passengers packed themselves on to nineteen carriages serviced by two engines and they made the journey to South Milford. Resplendent in their glory was Hudson, with Stephenson at his right side.

An endless round of speeches and toasts went on, Robert Stephenson's health was toasted then the crowd streamed back to the state-room of the Mansion House, where the Mayor of the day led off the dancing until four in the morning. The opening of the York Railway was indeed a large achievement especially to Hudson after six years of hard work. Hudson's prestige was at an all time high but in both politics and business he had made many enemies, Quakers were very suspicious of him with the handling of the companies finances. There was a host of other lines in the north of England designed to haul the coal from the south Durham coalmines to the sea outlets. These lines were the 'Clarence', 'The Durham & Sunderland', 'The Brandling Junction', 'The Durham Junction', and 'Stanhope & Tyne Railways'.

'The Great North of England Railway', did not prosper and it proceeded very slowly. The company engineer did not construct adequate bridges and Robert Stephenson had to come to their aid putting the finishing touches to the

Railway. Stephenson actually became their engineer, but on his own terms, one condition being that they drop all thought of preceding further with the second and northern half of the project between Darlington and Newcastle. At this time Robert Stephenson had his own problems as a major shareholder in the troubled Stanhope & Tyne Railway.

On February 26th1841, there was a half yearly meeting of the 'North Midland Company', and Hudson was nominated for election to the Board of Directors, but he declined the offer, he was too interested in the 'Great North of England Railway', and the Newcastle to Darlington route. People wondered at the time why the 'North Midland', with the prestige of Stephenson fared so badly against Hudson's line and the answer was clear to see, they had paid far too much for their land as opposed to Hudson.

The date was September 1843 Hudson had succeeded in a triple amalgamation of the Midlands Railway. People were now realizing the astuteness and importance of Hudson. York was fully aware of his wisdom where he had been nicknamed 'Gumsher Hudson', now London was calling him such names as 'The Yorkshire Balloon!' & 'Jupiter', and even 'The Railway Napoleon'. The Railway Times wrote 'I consider Hudson to be a shrewd and honest man', even comparing his power to that of Gladstone. After the hard won victories at the Midland meetings in August and September a lesser man would have taken a holiday – but not Hudson. An engineer and a promoter were just about to buy a whole railway putting the shares in their pockets, this was done by Hudson and Robert Stephenson when purchasing the Durham Junction Line in late Autumn 1843, for less than its original cost of construction. The next project was progressing the line to Newcastle then to Berwick. Finance was forthcoming from the shareholders of the Darlington Newcastle line. An obstacle stood in their way, 'The Tyne'.

Previously to this, the line ran only to Gateshead and now they accepted George Stephenson's scheme for a great bridge running at a high level across the river from Gateshead into Newcastle. The project was put forward at a price not exceeding £100,000 and a special Company had been put forward with George Stephenson on the board of Directors and Robert Stephenson as Engineer, and its dividend was guaranteed by the Newcastle Darlington Junction Company. Hudson travelled up and down the line from York making sure political matters at York were not abused. A new street was created called Micklegate to help the access to York Station, later the street was known as Hudson Street.

The High Level Bridge over the Tyne and the Berwick Railway progressed slowly. Rivalry was developing between York and North Midland also the Hull and Selby Railways. North of York there were towns with undeveloped docks, Hudson had thoughts of cargos of coal and iron ore being shipped, he also wished to build a line of watering places between Hull and Hartlepool by connecting up Filey and Bridlington with Scarborough, by a coastline. This caused problems with Selby and Hull railways as they naturally thought it was their territory. The Directors could not sustain a fight with Hudson unaided, and tended to stick close to the Manchester Leeds Railway, who were also hostile to the York and North Midland Railway. Sooner or later there would be a mighty conflict up and down Eastern England.

Rumours of Hudson buying the Great North of England were rife in the autumn of 1844, but it wasn't until May 1845 that Hudson made his move. The Railway Company was invited to lease their line to Hudson's group of Companies for five years at a guaranteed 10% on all classes of their shares and thereafter, the Newcastle & Darlington Junction Company would buy the whole line right out at the rate of £250 for every £100 share. The Great North of England shareholders would be paid off in 4% stock continuing to receive 10% in perpetuity on their existing capital. They stood to make an enormous advantage, in that in 1843, Great North of England £100 were quoted on the stock market at a discount of £40 from the beginning of 1845, when it was known Hudson was contemplating buying, they rose to a premium of £45 from £38. Hudson said that this was the hardest bargain he had ever been responsible for.

Total capital so far extended on the line was £1,300,000 and it would take 344 million new capitals to purchase it. The total income of the line to date was only £75,000 a year, yet the guaranteed rent he promised was £109,000 a year until 1847, and even more after that. In 1846, Hudson admitted in evidence before a Parliamentary Committee that he had paid more than market price for the line. He justified this by having more efficient management between York and Berwick; he then reduced prices on the line gaining public goodwill. Hudson added that he had no personnel interest in the purchase not holding a single share in the Great North of England at the time of its purchase. Hudson said that his interest really lay in rising shares in order to pay for the purchases. It was this that brought Hudson to eventual ruin.

In Hudson's present dealings, when he obtained unanimous agreement to the leases proved his hold on his three companies, Hull and Selby and the Great North of England lines. About this time Hudson raised the subscribing of a testimonial to George Stephenson in the form of a plate and the erection of a statue on the projected High Level Bridge over the Tyne, this actually applied also to Hudson, so two testimonials were planned. A story was told by Bridges Adams that Hudson himself drafted the appeal for his own testimonial, drawing up a list of subscribers with large sums next to their names. These included contractors and engineers. He instructed his secretary initially to send a list to the press after which they dare not refuse. He then asked all of the donations to be paid directly to his bankers. George Stephenson denounced this procedure saying that he intended writing a letter of refusal in the press, but other directors convinced him that this might affect the Railway shares.

Hudson travelled south to Westminster to monitor progress with the Railway Bill. On July 11th Lord Brougham complained that Hudson was working with a twelve Counsel power before the Committee on the London to York Line with obstructive purposes, and that he had interfered with the Committee. The merits of the London York bill had now being argued '*ad nauseam*' and the Committee's duties were finishing, speculation in company's shares were rife. An announcement on July 23rd; that with the casting votes of the Chairman the Bill was proved. The Bill had passed the standing order stage in the House of Lords without challenge. It was found that there were a lot of fictitious names and addresses and descriptions. A Bruce petition was introduced to enquire into allegations of the false signatures, but the bill still passed its third reading.

Later the petition was found to be well grounded, as follows. A charwoman's son had a contract as a subscriber for £12,000 worth of shares; a pensioner with an income of 10s weekly gave his rich brother's address and acquired £29,000 shares. £44,000 by persons with no property. Sadly at the very last stage of the Bill, the Lords Committee recommended that it should proceed no further until further investigations could be made. The seventy-day Committee, the Counsel, witnesses, and promoters in Parliament, together with outside speculators, found that Hudson's veto had fallen. The Midlands Railway was safe for another year when it could consolidate the east of England with its own Railway system.

There was a series of celebrations along the East of England in 1845; first at York Station on August 16th a reception was held good enough for Royalty, the Lord Mayor, Sheriff and the Dean of York. The Cathedral bells were rung, cannons fired, deafening cheers and music, welcomed the 'Railway King'. Hudson adored Whitby and right to the end of his life he was busy developing it as a watering place. The fisher people loved him and they hoped that he would build a line to transport their catches to markets. Hudson was entertained and flattered by the directors of the little Whitby & Pickering Railway. In 1846 when Hudson was at the height of his fame he met two other 'Kings', face to face Gawan Pierson, 'King of Goathland' and' Thomas Toddles, 'King of Staithes'. After Whitby, came Sunderland, there was a Conservative Banquet on October 21st 1845. For years businessmen had strived to create Sunderland as an important port, but had not succeeded – now Hudson was doing this in no time at all. The London to York Bill still haunted Hudson and proved very costly. The York & North Midland was charged with £30,000 and The Midland £50,000 as being their share of the costs. The Bill's passage through the Commons was assured if there were no changes. Hudson proposed to create a North South line of his own, to do this he would have to move south to London, he thereby took on the Chairmanship of the Eastern Counties Railway. This Railway was 150 miles long, one of the longest in the country carrying more goods than passengers. The Railway was badly managed and had a London terminus. Three million pounds had been spent on the line with only a dividend of 1% in July 1845.

Prior to moving to London Hudson bought 'The Durham & Sunderland Railway' for £270,000 *(double market value)*. Robert Stephenson's Railway, 'Pontop & South Shields' where at Jarrow Slake on the Tyne, he built a fine new Dock for £200,000, he also leased to the 'Newcastle & Darlington' Company the Hartlepool Dock and Railway, which linked the Town with the main line. The *Times* declared Hudson had secured an almost entire command of the Northern Railways in the County of Durham. It was calculated that he would be able to ship the coals of the great colliery owners such as Londonderry and the Earl of Durham and also the Hetton Coal Company at Sunderland. It was said that one of the major blunders of Hudson's career was the Chairmanship of the Eastern Counties Railway; it was thought impossible to make a profit. Strategically the Eastern Counties Railway was an unusual partner for the Midland and York, and the North Midland Railways. Because of the Alliance, Hudson's Companies were more vulnerable and hard to knit together. By the end of 1843, railway mania grew more pronounced, engineers such as Brunel, Locke, Rennie, and Vignotles found that they were in urgent demand. George Stephenson was now retired and living at Tapton House but his son, Robert, was connected with 34 separate lines. Hudson often called at Stephenson's offices at 24 Great George Street, Westminster.

The demand for labour of all kinds increased the price of iron doubled; Solicitors, Stockbrokers and Estate Agents were all in demand. A return called by Parliament to show the number of people who had subscribed to railway shares of £2000; these were recorded as 900 Lawyers, 364 Bankers, 257 Clergymen, and 157 Members of Parliament. At Leeds, four share markets were opened and York had its own Stock Exchange. Literary intellectuals were also very impressed with Hudson, two of the most interesting were Emily and Ann Bronte, and both sent small amounts for investments. There were of course exceptions in the family, Charlotte tried to persuade her sisters to sell when the going was good, and both lost money with the slump. George Stephenson said from his retirement at Tapton that Hudson had became too great for him now, he went on to say that he had made Hudson a rich man but he would soon care for nobody unless he could make money by them. The amalgamation of the lines north of York was

98

accomplished in two stages; the first of these was the ratification by Parliament of the purchase of the Great North of England Railway by the Newcastle and Darlington Junction Company. The new company was renamed in September 1846, as the York and Newcastle Railway. The first meeting of the new Company was September 1846. There was an issue of 159,000 new shares at £25 which would make the new company £6,625,000. Hudson had made a pledge to buy out every holder of a hundred pound share in the Great North of England, at a price of £250 before 1851.

The Queen

On July 5th 1847, young Queen Victoria and the Prince Consort travelled on the Eastern Counties Railway to Cambridge where she attended the installation of the Chancellor of the University. Hudson had the opportunity to put on a flamboyant display. A special train was fitted out for the occasion. The Queen, looking very regal in a transparent cottage bonnet and peach blossomed satin dress. She bade Mr. Hudson good-morning whereon he guided her into the pavilion filled with elegantly dressed woman. From there he escorted her to the Royal carriage and presented her with a beautifully executed map of the line, and illuminated copies of the timetable of the Royal train. The carriage was coloured white and gold outside. The linings and furniture were of French gray satin. The roof was fluted with the same material and the carriage hung with the fairest and freshest favours of flora. On arrival at Cambridge, Hudson leapt out of his carriage and quickly opened the Queen's carriage door. The Queen took hold of his arm and he escorted her into the pavilion, preceded by the Earl Marshall, the Duke of Norfolk. Later, Prince Albert on behalf of the Queen conveyed her Majesty's gracious acknowledgements of her entire satisfaction of her comfort and well-being.

Downturn

Hudson's calculations were made on expectation that the year 1847 was the worst possible year of the trade depression. He thought that as trade revived prosperity would follow. Happenings occurred throughout England and the world that Hudson had discounted. Revolution and riot were rife throughout Europe. Not even the strongest constitution could withstand the coming storm. In April 1848 Hudson became ill and was confined to bed with a digestive problem, which later affected his heart and caused attacks of '*Angina Pectoris*'. His Parliamentary speeches were affected, one, he actually did make was on behalf of Sunderland, where one third of the countries shipping was constructed. In the middle of May, Robert Davies after completing twenty years as Town Clerk at York retired. Hudson missed his old friend whom he could trust to guide the machinery of local government in York. In August–September 1848, Hudson had to repay £400,000 that he had had to borrow from banks on behalf of his various companies. He achieved this, but it left his reserves seriously deflated and future dividends were in jeopardy. Rumours leaked about the massive repayment and it started panic throughout Hudson's shareholders. By October 27th The York and North Midland £50 share had fallen from £62 to £46, York Newcastle and Berwick £25 from 30¾ to £23, Midland £100 stock from £93 to £73, Eastern Counties £20 shares £14 3/8 to £12 5/8. The Railway stock throughout the county was also affected. Hudson once again suffered with his digestive problems and his financial statements were delayed until November 14th. For the moment the shares were checked but there was an obvious storm brewing and investors settled down to await the next set of accounts. The S & D Railway Company had rather declined from its original glory and the directors wished Hudson to place it in his care, and by November 1848 an agreement had been made with Hudson.

A notice appeared in the press that the line was to be leased to York, Newcastle and Berwick at a guarantee of 9% on capital, the North British Railway had also changed their minds and approached Hudson, but now conditions were different, and in any case Hudson could not now raise the capital necessary. The capital expended on 'The King's' four railways was enormous and up to the end of 1848 the Capital accounts were as follows, York and North Midland, £4,620,000, the York Newcastle and Berwick £7,245,000, the Midland Amalgamated Railways in the winter of 1843 was £6,245,000 at the end of 1848 it was £14,000,000, the Eastern Counties Company had grown from £3,804,000 to £13,139,000 by 1849. The 'Railway King' had spent just about £30,000,000 capital most going to guaranteed dividends on leases and shareholders. Now no more capital was forthcoming from any source. Each of the four half-yearly meetings in 1849, spelt trouble for the 'Railway King'. One remarkable fact was that he had lent £150,000 of the shareholders money to Sunderland Dock Company without Parliamentary sanction. He also had trouble with the strangulation of Hull shipping by the Danish blockade.

In January there was a rumour of his impending resignation. Matters for Hudson went from bad to worse and on August 12th 1848, George Stephenson died in his 68th year. Stephenson and Hudson had been associates since the 'Railway Mania', started in 1835, but he had lived more or less in retirement since 1845. The passing of Stephenson proved an ill omen for Hudson. The 'Railway King' was put further and further under pressure, as one after the other the discrepancies surfaced. What made matters worse was the fact that Hudson's financial statements of accounts were not properly recorded, especially the entries in the purchase account. There was no dates or any times of any transactions. James Richardson and Robert Davies had signed any cheque laid before them. Eventually the 'Prance', report was published which blasted any good name that Hudson had left, many wished the 'Railway King' to be prosecuted for the violation of the 85th Clause of the Companies Act. The press was devastating, with, 'Mr. Hudson will not escape us', and 'Mr. Hudson has duped thousands'. Hudson was dragged in front of the Tribunal of the Eastern Counties Railway, Mr. Cash, the Chairman questioned Hudson relentlessly, "Didst thou ever, after the accountant had made up the yearly accounts, alter any of the figures? Hudson replied very subdued and after hesitation, "Well, I may have perhaps of added a thousand or two to the next accounts. "Didst thou alter the accounts to say £10,000 or even £40,000?" the Quaker added. Hudson replied nervously, "Maybe not as much as that. Cash let Hudson off the hook and never pressed the point, he said, "...thou should go home and write down these amounts," – much to Hudson's relief. Out of £545.714 distributed in dividends from January 4th 1845, to July 4th 1848, £115,278 was procured by the alteration of traffic accounts, and £205,294 by wrongly charging capital accounts, making a total of £320,572, which was not subject to dividends. In fact out of £545,714 distributed in dividends from January 4th 1845, to July 4th. 1848, £115,278 was procured by the alteration of traffic accounts and £205,294 by wrongly charging the capital account making a total of £320,572, which was not subject to dividends. Out of £545,714 only £225,142 had been earned and therefore subject to dividends.

The Observer recorded at this time that for four years £13,000,000, the property of the company, has been at the mercy of Hudson and Waddington with which they did as they choose, making and unmaking dividends, traffic. capital, and revenue, pocketing cheque's with no authority, re-directing sums to their own accounts, they even charged hotel bills to the company. Hudson's friends at Sunderland rallied loyally behind him, but to no avail. On May 4th a letter of resignation was forthcoming from Hudson. The 'King's' brother-in-law, Richard Nicholson, was not made of, 'as sterner stuff' as the other Yorkists and the Prance report had implicated him also. After a meeting on May 5th this was the last time he was seen. On the night of May 8th he left his house at Clifton and walked along the bank of the Ouse, to Marygate and he was never seen alive again. His body was recovered from the river the following day.

The news reached Hudson at Newby Park where he was struck with grief. Within days of receiving this news Hudson had to attend the House of Commons. A petition had been presented that he had bribed his fellow members of Parliament. On the evening of May 17th Hudson stood to answer the charges; at first he was unable to speak he stood, his large head lightly covered with gray hair, his broad forehead and penetrating eyes looking pathetic, like an overgrown schoolboy. He finally began hesitatingly saying he never signed a company cheque, saying he merely presided over them. He went on to say that he had taken a sanguine view of everything. If it were determined what should go to revenue and what should go to capital, there would be a clearer picture. The majority heard his speech in stony silence. An investigative committee uncovered a web of deceit. One item alone showed Hudson himself had kept £37,350, paid for the purchase of land in fact it was £31,000. The landowners concerned were the Duke of Northumberland, £10,000, Earl of Tankerville, £4000, Earl Grey £5000, Lady Mary Stanley £2000, Earl of Carlisle, £7000, Sir M.W. Ridley £3000. These amounts had simply been taken and paid into Hudson's own account at the York Union Bank. Suddenly this money resurfaced and was repaid with interest. Similar practice had happened with contractors when another £40,000 was deposited to Hudson's account. Other accounts had been manipulated to the tune of £121,925 just quoting one in particular. Early in January 1850 Hudson consented to pay in instalments a sum of over £100,000, in settlement of all claims made against him by the company. This had its good and bad points for Hudson. Subscribers was at least getting some of their investment back, but it appeared an admission of guilt. On June 20th 1850, the Sunderland Dock was opened, one of Hudson's greatest achievements. There were fifty thousand spectators, cannons were fired and there were scenes of rejoicing. Hudson was in his element making speeches, pointing to the High Level Bridge, at Newcastle and now this magnificent dock. This occasion was short lived for the 'Railway King' as one after another Chancery cases alighted. The Solicitor General and the Master of the Rolls decided against him and finally Newby Park had to be sold. Hudson negotiated and made an offer of settlement with the directors of the York and Midland in 1854, after which no more claims would be pressed against him. For a total of £72,697, he had already paid £26,083, and the balance was now £46,614.

No sooner did he get this debt settled then a further one emerged – that he had bribed Members of Parliament, then a further one emerged when contracting to supply 20,000 tons of iron. This was heard on February 18th 1854, when a French Count sued him for £4000 damages. This recent expense meant that by the Autumn of 1854 he had fallen into arrears with his payments to York and North Midland Company, his Parliamentary immunity protected him from his creditors while the Commons was in session, but in recess he had to resort to all kind of evasive action to stay at liberty. Hudson found it impossible to retrieve any of his fortune doing business with foreign rail companies, and the pressures of merely living was enormous, subsequently for a little peace he decided to go abroad, on the 12th August 1855 he left for Spain. On reaching San Sebastian he had a violent attack of his health problem, which confined him to bed for months. Very despondent, Hudson returned to England and Sunderland where he promised to attend better to his constituent's problems as their MP, if he was reelected. He was again returned as their representative in Parliament, where he worked hard on their behalf; in recess he went to Paris to avoid his creditors.

Hudson's wife managed to salvage a little money out of their wrecked affairs and she lived in lodgings in Belgravia, London. In November 1857, she was robbed of clothes and jewellery to the value of £200, because of this she was traumatized with grief. To add to all this, her second son, John, who was having a brilliant military career as an officer in the '6th Carabineers' serving in India, had been killed in the Indian Mutiny. This was a terrible blow to the family. There was a further setback when their one remaining enterprise, the 'Sunderland Dock Company', which Hudson had £60,000 invested, was reported to be doing badly. Lord Londonderry and other coal owners appeared jealous of the docks and started boycotting the facilities. This was also the time of Seaham Harbour, Jarrow, Middlesborough and Hartlepool all touting for trade, so the dividend at Sunderland could not be maintained.

Hudson lost his seat at Sunderland and had to go quickly to Paris where he lived in exile to escape his creditors. In the autumn of 1859 Robert Stephenson died leaving his seat vacant at Whitby. The Whitby people loved Hudson, but he dare not venture back to England as his creditors would have him, and besides he was penniless. His old enemy H. S. Thompson of Moat Hall carried the seat. Hudson travelled from one Channel port to another living in cheap hotels, eating where and when he could. This was not doing his old medical condition any good at all and he was steadily growing shabbier and poorer. Creditors still hounded him relentlessly wishing to foreclose on his Whitby Estate. The Sunderland Dock Company was wound up and Hudson's shares were worthless. Charles Dickens later came across Hudson when he was travelling to France, speaking to his friend Dickens said, "I feel I should know that man". The year was 1863 and Hudson was taking leave of a friend, he was shabbily dressed and waving his high hat in a desolate and sad manner. Dickens was informed that it was Hudson and he was amazed. This fact was mentioned in Dickens' 'Life of Dickens', which he later wrote.

Hudson failed because of his own faults, but only he could have accomplished what he did. In the early nineteenth century, England required an efficient Rail system quickly to take advantage of the next twenty-five years, when most other countries in the world were struggling. Hudson succeeded with the help of Stephenson, and other engineers, to do just this; they produced a very efficient system capable of keeping England ahead of the rest. Hudson was a rogue in many ways but a scrupulous, unselfish man could never have produced the railway. It needed a man with unusual moral values and whose ambition was success. An interpretation of the 'Railway King's' character was given in a report by Dr. Robert Saudek, who was Europe's leading graphologist who, on sight of a specimen of Hudson's handwriting, and without any knowledge whatsoever who's writing it was gave the following analysis...

"Here is a man of tremendous temperament, nervous, irritable, neurotic and impatient—with himself, as well as others—gifted with farsightedness, grasping things at a moment's notice, ever ready for combinations – lacks the ability to make himself easily understood, as his thinking would be faster than he could speak, and his instructions could be misinterpreted"

After Hudson's downfall much of the report made sense. On June 8th 1865, Hudson finally returned to England and Whitby to contest the Parliamentary seat there after the dissoltion of Parliament that year. Hudson, in an address to a large public meeting, promised to take 'West Cliff Estate' back out of the hands of the Railway Company and develop it for the town. Forty-eight hours before the poll, the Sheriff's Officer entered Hudson's bedroom early on Sunday morning July 8th and arrested him for debt. Hudson was placed in the unsanitary old town prison at York Castle, where he stayed for three months. His creditors, mainly due to campaigning by the Whitby people, finally released him and he remained always in their hearts. By now his health had completely gone and he only lived for a little peace. His real friends thought it was about time Hudson and his family had that peace, and subsequently Hudson and his wife were allowed to live quietly in retirement at 87 Churton Street, London.

To the day of Hudson's death his spirit was fresh and alive and he quite enjoyed talking of his experiences and eventual downfall. His eventual death came in the winter of 1871. He had come north to York to visit some old friends staying at the house of J. L. Foster, one of his oldest friends. He became very ill and also had attacks of angina. Hudson crept back to his wife in London where on December 14th he died. His remains were returned to York where they toured the City and across Lendal Bridge for the last time. Hudson's family and friends were in close attendance. Close, *(faithful secretary,* Cabrey *(Engineer)*, and J. L. Foster *(editor)*. The procession toured the valley of Derwent and the Wolds. He was finally interned in the churchyard at Scrayingham. These days the tall grass hides the grave and the words carved on the gravestone are obliterated.

There's a bad time going, boys,
A bad time going!
Railway shares have seemed to be
A sink fore! Men's property   **Punch, 1848**
In the bad times going.
Lines, which used to quarrel then,
To prove whose purse was stronger,
Shall be controlled by honest men...
Wait a little longer!"

George Hudson at the height of his fame:

Hudsons old Shop, and how it is today

JOHN SMEATON
(Lighthouse Builder)

John Smeaton was making important discoveries before the time of the Industrial Revolution in England – as if to test the resolve of the British people for change and advancement. Smeaton was born in 1724 at *Austhorpe*, Leeds, the son of a very eminent and prosperous lawyer, William Smeaton who never thought for a moment that his son, John, would become a great engineer and a builder/designer of lighthouses; bridges; canals; and harbours. He also became a Fellow of the Royal Society.

Smeaton wished his son to follow in his footsteps and become a lawyer, an occupation that had supplied him with a very prosperous life. The difference between John Smeaton and his following associates like Stephenson; Brunel; Telford; Fairbairn; Rennie and Brindley, was that they had a constant struggle with adversity and all had to educate themselves, initially scraping to earn money to even nourish themselves. Brindley was more or less illiterate all of his life. Smeaton was different, having education and finance at his disposal from his early beginnings, all he had to do was to overcome the pressures put on him by his father to follow in his footsteps in the profession as a lawyer.

Austhorpe was a beautiful house, which had been built by Smeaton's grandfather in the parish of Whitkirk. John Smeaton was born 8th June, 1724, a brother born 1727 died at five years of age making John an only child - although a baby girl was born in 1732, but died when she was a year old. There were no other children where John grew up; consequently he grew up with many older people's habits. From an early age he designed and made things, even at six he studied a local windmill and just what made it work, then constructed a toy one of his own, climbing to the top of his fathers barn so it got the maximum wind in its sails. Basically John's taste was not toys but machinery.

William Smeaton eventually succumbed to his son's interest thinking that if John was so interested in Engineering design he would have a workshop and every tool imaginable to further his interest. John used the tools to great effect making other and better tools for all kinds of uses and complicated functions.

Smeaton was given early tuition in reading and writing and he showed an interest in mathematics from an early age. When he was old enough, John attended Leeds Grammar School where it was found he had a natural aptitude for mathematics and in particular geometry. It was also found that he was very good at drawing. When he was sixteen, John left school. Knowing fully that his father wished him to succeed him, in the family legal business he joined the firm studying law, knowing that it would please his father, also knowing that he could make a humbler living in mechanics, and his love for the latter far outweighed the legal profession.

There was a coal mine very near to Smeaten's home and it was here where he first saw a steam engine, this was at Garforth. One of the main problems with early mining for coal was that after rain most of the mine would be flooded. Thomas Newcomen invented a primitive steam engine about this time just for this purpose and this was the engine taking Smeaton's interest. He sketched it from every angle then went home and designed and produced a working model of the engine. To try the capabilities of the machine he tried it on his father's fishpond – it did so well it killed all of his father's fish! His father was not amused but he marvelled at his son's genius and inventiveness in constructing the engine just on sight of the engine at Garforth. Solely to please his father John attended his office in Leeds, where his tasks were mainly copying legal documents and learning general law. In the evenings, John enjoyed his workshop where he worked until late at night. John's father felt that his son would never learn law based at Leeds, consequently, thinking that he would create more interest for his son, he arranged for him to go to London where he could attend the courts at Westminster Hall – well away from his workshop.

John Smeaton left for London in the autumn of 1742. Smeaton loved his father tremendously and no one could say that he didn't give his father's profession a try, working hard in legal circles during the day but in his own time in the evenings, John attended libraries, reading endlessly on the subjects that interested him – mostly mechanics. Smeaton missed his workshop, mainly for putting his ideas into practice, so much so that he sat down and wrote a well-presented letter to his father informing him that he wished to give up the profession of lawyer saying that he wished to follow a career as a mechanical engineer. William Smeaton showed that he was a reasonable man and that he also loved his son, he also admired the way his son had tried in London and, even though disappointed, he wrote giving his son permission to follow his own interests as a career. Not only did he do this he awarded him a generous allowance to help him with his living costs. The allowance was *very* generous and carried on for the rest of Smeaton's life. William Smeaton had played a very important part in the discoveries of John Smeaton and without this help England may never have heard of the marvellous discoveries of John Smeaton. On receipt of his father's letter, John was overjoyed and he quickly resigned his lawyer's position and entered the service of an instrument maker to learn the trade. He also attended meetings of the Royal Society and through the Society met many famous scientists. Even as early as 26th July in 1750, John Smeaton read his first paper where he described improvements to the mariner's compass. A year later, in 1751, he invented an instrument for measuring the speed of ships at sea. Other papers read to the Royal Society included one on air pumps, another one on pulleys and tackle and yet another one describing steam engines. Three years later in 1754 Smeaton was elected FRS. A high distinction for one so young and a pointer to the esteem other members held for him. This was also the year when he began learning French, mainly to read French language mechanic books; he also began to take a keen interest in the civil engineering of docks and canals, harbours, drainage, and navigation safety.

Belgium and Holland was thought to be more advanced than England in these fields and Smeaton decided to travel there in 1754. He travelled cheaply by foot and canal barge, noting and sketching Dutch dykes and the canal system. He thought the docks and harbours of Amsterdam were amazing. London did not have any, then relying mainly on tides for the ship to go alongside the wharf and later, for leaving. In Amsterdam the docks were kept full by means of locks, ignoring tides. The notes and sketches Smeaton made were of immense use, not only to himself but also to the country in general. He used these effectively later in his life. Smeaton always had a great respect for the power of the sea always realizing that docks and sea walls had to be constructed with great strength to withstand storms tides and the overall power of the sea.

On December 2nd 1755, Eddystone Lighthouse caught fire – it had been happily helping shipping on the Rock for forty-six years. On looking at a map of the English Channel, the south coast of Cornwall and West Devon form a great bay showing the lizard and Start Point. If a line was drawn between these two it would pass very near to a reef and rocks lying roughly fourteen miles south S. West, of Plymouth and called Eddystone. The reef, which consists of several large rocks, laying twelve to fourteen feet from the water at low tide, and covered completely with the spring high tide. This hazard laid in the track of ships using the channel especially those heading for Plymouth.

Over the years the Eddystone has been responsible for hundreds of ships with valuable cargos being wrecked and lost, not to mention thousands of lives of seamen. Prior to 1696 it was generally thought that nothing could be done to highlight this death trap during the night and indeed private owners had to place their own lights on the cliff-top to guide their own ships away from the hazard. To own a lighthouse as early as 1700 was very lucrative, as the owner was allowed to collect 'dues', from the owners of passing shipping? Although a financially sound proposition, it was thought to be virtually impossible to erect a lighthouse on Eddystone Rock, and a lot of clever engineers of the day had kept well away from the project.

Henry (Whimsical) Winstanley lived in Essex in 1696 he very much-enjoyed playing jokes on people especially with mechanical devices. Winstanley applied for a licence to put up a Lighthouse on Eddystone and collect the 'dues'. The application was granted, possibly because the task was so hard and a joker like Winstanley would fail, anyway it was thought a dream. This dream became a reality when he built the lighthouse, to date, the best, the world had ever seen. It was made of wood and held by twelve iron posts fixed into the rock; it had an eight-sided tower with a balustrade and open gallery. Eight posts supported the dome, gallery, and lantern. The whole object being seventy feet high. Slogans were seen on the tower like, *'Pax in Bello'*, and *'Glory be to God'*. Above this was a fantastic array of pulleys and hoists and finally a railed platform and flagpole flying a huge flag, with a weather vane to top it all.

In November 1698 it showed a light to warn shipping, and often the crew could not get home for two weeks, they even went hungry on occasions but all the time the light kept saving lives. In 1703 Winstanley was at the lighthouse overseeing repairs and on the evening of 26th November there was a great storm when terrific damage was done to all seaports, especially in the south of England. People in Plymouth wondered if the lighthouse had withstood the storm, and to their amazement nothing could be seen of it! It had completely blown away with everyone in it. All that was left was twelve irons in the rock and a piece of chain, which was embedded in the rock – so much for the first Eddystone Lighthouse. The second lighthouse arrived three years later; at least shipping was warned away from the rock by a light from July 1706, although the lighthouse was not complete until 1709. Over the period when there was no lighthouse, there were many disasters, one in particular being *'Winchelsea'*, sailing homeward to England with a rich cargo and many passengers from the Virginias, America. This disaster shocked the Nation and it recognized the need for a new lighthouse. It was a Cornishman who built the second lighthouse, John Rudyard who owned a silk shop on Ludgate Hill. Again the construction was made of wood but it offered a resistance to the waves by being conical. It was built of stout timbers, like the ocean going vessels, and it withstood storms and buffeting for forty-six years. A team of keepers renewed the light in shifts; candles were used to produce the light. This, it was thought, caused the roof area to become completely dry and brittle and it sadly caught fire.

How the fire started was not clear, one of the keepers went to renew the candles at 2 am and found the lantern area filled with smoke, on opening the door it fanned the flames, which became fierce. The three keepers between them tried to fight the flames with buckets of water, without much hope of putting the fire out – until finally they had to take refuge on the rocks. The weather at the time was good and the sea calm and the fire had been seen from the shore. A boat put to sea to rescue the men, one being ninety-four. On reaching the shore one of the keepers took to his heels and was never seen again. The old man of ninety-four insisted that, as he looked up at the flames in the roof, some molten rock poured down his throat. Fourteen days later he died and they found a flat piece of lead weighing seven ounces in his stomach.

Mr. Weston, mainly to collect the 'Dues', financed a new lighthouse and he wished it to be quickly re-built. His first enquiry was made to the president of the Royal Society, who was the Earl of Macclesfield. The Earl strongly recommended John Smeaton for the job he had a great knowledge of mechanics and on his record had always produced quality work. The Earl's recommendation was good enough for Weston and he sent a message to Smeaton, who was at this time in Scotland. Weston did not interview John but asked him point-blank to build a lighthouse. The message took a month to reach Smeaton who was busy on another project. Thinking it was a re-build job he wasn't very keen but on finding it was a complete new lighthouse, he took up the challenge and hurried back to London. Weston's letter had said *Thou art the man to do it'*. Smeaton set to work studying the problem of the third lighthouse. He made a lengthy study of the previous ones then decided that this one would be built of stone. No one thought it possible to build the lighthouse of stone. Smeaton knew he needed a heavy building to withstand the battering – later he would be proved right. Smeaton studied the London curbstones, which, because they were interlocked with each other, never moved, and he decided to 'dove-tail' his stone accordingly. The base of the building would be weighted down with heavy rocks. No stone would be able to move on its own and would be firmly held by every other one. Smeaton experimented with cement until he found one that quickly set and was not affected by salt. He then made a complete drawing of the building even before going to see Eddystone Reef.

It was March 1756, when Smeaton set out for Plymouth and it took him six days. While at Plymouth, Smeaton called to see Josiah Jessup, he was a foreman shipwright and had a great knowledge of the sea and ships. On hearing that Smeaton had decided to build the lighthouse of stone, he thought it impossible but admitted if it was possible it would withstand the greatest of storms. Jessup later gave Smeaton much help with his construction. Smeaton now proposed to visit the rock; there were strong winds around the channel at the time so it was April before Smeaton managed it. The breakers were battering right over the rock so it was impossible to get onto it getting an idea of the ferocity of the sea in the area. Three days later he returned and this time managed to get on, and he stayed for two hours. On three other occasions he tried to get back on but found it impossible until the weather changed, when he made measurements and made sketches. One evening, he worked by candlelight until 9pm. Eventually, John was aware of every inch of the reef. Smeaton began to make preparations back at Plymouth at a place called Mill Bay where he started shaping and storing his stones. He instructed the making of a modification to the landing area on the rock, he then set out for London to report to his employer Weston. When he arrived in London, Smeaton constructed a model exactly based on his proposed lighthouse, making adjustments as he went along. On completion, Smeaton showed it to Weston and also the Lords of the Admiralty, all were completely satisfied, if not amazed at the engineering that would go into the project. Smeaton again set off for Plymouth, on the way ordering the Portland stone, engaged the workmen, hired transport, too and from Eddystone, finally he bought all of the stores and provisions and tools. Josiah Jessup was appointed his first assistant.

On the 31st August *1756*, he began the project. Landing again on the rock, he marked out the centre of the building. Some days, because of the tide, no work could be done. Other days they managed about six hours a day cutting a base into the hard rock where the Portland stone would fit. All had to be done by hand hammer and chisel, quickly before the start of winter. It was really hard work but the dovetails had to be completed exactly, these would be the strength of the base and by November they had completed this first phase and returned to Plymouth. It took them four days to do this and many on the shore thought they were lost, as the sea was blowing an almighty gale which had blown them as far as the Bay of Biscay – it took tremendous courage and seamanship to get back to Plymouth. The rest of the winter was spent at Mill Bay, dressing the rest of the Portland stones to the exact size. Each one weighed upwards of two tons. Over the winter, 450 tons were cut to size and fitted into the next, as they would be on Eddystone. Finally, each stone was numbered, each one ready for transportation to the rock.

It was June 1757, and on the twelfth of that month the first stone was laid on the rock and it weighed 2.25 tons. Next day the first course of four stones was laid taking into account that the reef sloped. The following courses allowed for this, the second course having thirteen stones the third twenty-five stones. Eventually a perfect, circular course was reached containing 61 stones. Work progressed well because of Smeaton's planning, especially in the stone yard where every stone was first tried in sequence then, within that sequence, transported to the rock, fitted and cemented after fitting within the dovetails. Two holes were bored in each stone and oak treenails driven to the stone below, nothing being left to chance. After six courses, there was a level platform above the waves.

One day Smeaton was testing the platform and fell over on to the rocks, dislocating his thumb, he bravely and painfully jerked his thumb back into place, there being no medical help, then carried on with the work as if nothing had happened. Nine courses were laid before winter 1757, and before returning to Plymouth they left a converted boat to shine a warning to shipping, which more often than not had to seek shelter because of storms, the weather was a good test for the part finished lighthouse.

When spring arrived it wasn't possible to get to the rock until May 12th. 1758. Smeaton and his men found it had not even moved a fraction of an inch and the cement had set completely. By September 24 courses were finished bringing the height to 35 feet. The base being complete they started on the walls, which were 26 inches thick, these being the storeroom and living area. That particular winter was good and before retiring they completed the lower storeroom and up to the roof where they put on a temporary cover. The following year, 1759, was very stormy and they did not get to the rock until July 5th. By August, the masonry was finished, there were 46 courses of stones, and the height was 70 feet. The iron work, balcony; and lantern came next, ending with the fitting of the gilt ball which crowned the whole edifice – which Smeaton fixed himself. Smeaton never left until everything was complete fixing the windows himself.

On the 16th. October 1759, the light shone for the first time and Smeaton breathed a sigh of relief and satisfaction. He inscribed round the upper wall *'except the Lord build the house, they labour in vain that build it'.*
In 1848 the Harbour Master of Plymouth making an annual inspection of the lighthouse found it had leaned one quarter of an inch towards the Northeast. Feeling apprehensive in that even a quarter of an inch from the perpendicular was important, he referred to Smeaton's journal of the times reading,
'...This day the Eddystone Lighthouse has thank God been completed, it is I believe perfect, except that it inclines a quarter of an inch from the perpendicular to the north east'.
Ninety years after Smeaton completed the lighthouse, it still stands as a tribute to his skills.

In 1877 it was found that the reef had been affected by erosion and seawater, accordingly another tower had to be built 120 feet away in 1882. Smeaton's tower was taken down stone by stone and re-erected on Plymouth Hoe; the solid stone base still stands on the rock, unaffected by weather and the strong waves of the Channel. The tower at Hoe is a tribute to a great engineer. John Smeaton was awarded a gold medal *(highest possible award)* by the Royal

Society in 1759. Smeaton also built 40 more efficient water mills, and four windmills in various areas of England. He built four bridges, three being in Scotland at Perth; a seven arch, at Coldstream and Banff, and one at Hexham in the north of England, *(the latter being his only failure)*. Later in his life he wrote many narratives the main one being *The Eddystone Lighthouse*, and his drawings of the lighthouse were exquisite.

Like most people who put work before health, he was afflicted with stomach ulcers, which later probably led to him having a stroke. What is certain about John Smeaton is that over the many years that Eddysone Lighthouse stood on the rock, it saved thousands of lives. Now standing at Plymouth Hoe it is a great tribute to him and will never be forgotten.

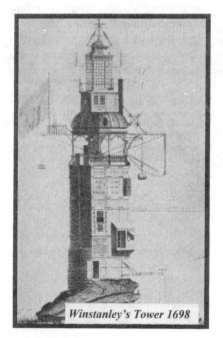

Winstanley's Tower 1698

Rudyard's Tower 1709

Eddystone (Douglas, with stump of Smeatons lighthouse)

The unique process of making the base, with dovetail:

ROBERT SURTEES
(Wrote a History of Durham)

Robert Surtees furnished historians with the brilliant, 'Surtees History of Durham'.

Before Robert was even born his parents had been married nearly eighteen years and two other children had died in infancy. Robert was born in the parish of St. Mary's, in the South Bailey, Durham on the 1st April 1779. His baptism being registered in St. Mary's the following day. The Church commonly known as St. Mary-Le-Bow. The baptism was also recorded at Bishop Middleham Church. Robert spent his childhood at his parent's hereditary seat at Mainsforth, in the County of Durham. His early impressions of the area were of quiet and rural elegance. Robert's early memories, which he delighted in talking about, were the happy days spent fishing at Cornforth beck.

In May 1786, Robert was sent to public school where it was hoped he would find his own level. The school was situated at Houghton-le-Spring not too near or far from home. At this time the Reverend William Fleming MA of Queens College, Oxford, was teaching and to whom Robert acknowledged as, '…owing a great full tribute of respect'.

Mr. Raine, Surtees' valued friend, [who later helped to compile much information], stated that on one occasion they were at Hexham together when they came upon a monument to his old master. He was very moved, speaking of him affectionately. Surtees' first two years was spent getting well grounded in Latin but not starting with arithmetic until 1788, then Greek in December the same year. He was also very familiar with the language of the classics. Robert Surtees had an extraordinary power of memory, which came in very handy with Latin verse. He had also studied general antiquities and the topographical history of his country, carefully preserving any documents that came his way. Surtees also had a great love for coins and travelled to Sunderland and Durham in search of them, Roman being his preference.

Even as early as 1790-91 Surtees was preparing his data for writing the 'History of Durham', checking on ownership of properties; family histories; ancient verse; in fact anything which would help him to compile the same.

113

Robert, during these years had two close friends also attending Houghton School they were Ralph and William Robinson of Herrington, he spent much of his holiday periods with the family culminating in Robert marrying their sister. Surtees finally left Houghton School in 1793 and was placed under the care of Doctor Bristow who at Neasdon, near London, prepared young men for university. It was here that he met Reginald Heber *(Bishop of Calcutta);* Sir Wastell Brisco of Crofton Hall, Cumberland and the Pierrepoints, sons of the Earl of Manvers.

On the 14th October 1795, Surtees matriculated at Oxford; and on the 20th October 1796, entered as a commoner at Christchurch His fellow collegian was William Ward Jackson Esq. of Normanby, in Yorkshire. Surtees' tutor was the Reverend M. Marsh who was later Canon of Salisbury. During his stay at Oxford Surtees was very studious, he read Herodotus; the whole of Thucydides; Euripides; The Hellenics & Anabasis of Xenophon; Diodorus Siculus; Polybius, and many others. At the end of each term he gained credits at the examinations. Besides the College lectures on mathematics, logic and rhetoric he also attended those of the University in anatomy and natural philosophy.

The course of study was accomplished with some absences because of his parents' illness – as well as his own. He exerted himself in the composition of what was called Lent Verses. Each copy having from twelve to twenty lines. It was an annual exercise at Christ's Church, on subjects chosen by the writers, and six copies were usually expected from the competitors, subject to the eye of the Censor on which he thought worth public reading. Surtees produced six copies of verses of which four received the distinction of being publicly read, which was a great achievement.

In the spring of 1782, Surtees was called from Oxford as his mother had an alarming illness; she sadly died on the 10th. March 1782, in her sixty-first year, being buried close by, at Bishop Middleham Church. Surtees and his friend Mr. Pemberton took the degree of Bachelor of Arts. They both became members of the Middle Temple; one of the advantages of this was having a good dinner, with a bottle of good old Domus-Wine. Mr. Surtees time at the Middle Temple was sadly interrupted when he had to leave, in 1797 because of his father's death on the 14th. July 1797. Robert, now twenty-four, became established for life at Mainsforth Hall; his father was buried at Bishop Middleham beside his mother.

The manner in which Surtees wrote the Durham History was amazing, he never sat down to write, but wandered about his front garden deep in thought then returned to his library and hastily wrote down his findings. His mind was filled rapidly and his pen could not record quickly enough his creative thoughts, resulting in his writing being legible to him alone. When sending his 'copy', to the press the different paragraphs and sentences were generally pinned and numbered together. The Compositor had problems deciphering his writing and Surtees was often amused, but with his photographic memory, correction was not difficult. His 'copy', was never available until absolutely needed, but he could always provide for the current day's work.

Correspondence started at this time between Robert Surtees and the celebrated Walter Scott, Surtees having started the exchange of letters between the two great men. Surtees thought information in his possession would be useful in the new edition of the "Border Minstrelsy". Over the period of the exchange of letters, the subjects discussed were ballad poetry, border history and tradition, which were thought extremely important as an alternative source of the Durham History. Scott's first letter to Surtees is dated 1806 *(Selkirk);* Surtees reply is dated 8th. December 1806. The letter by Surtees requires explanation. It starts by giving a border ballad on the feud between the Ridleys and Featherstone's from the recitation of an old woman of Alston Moor, accompanied with explanations and historical notes to determine dates of the transaction. Scott was delighted with the contribution to his collection and was satisfied to the validity of the piece, introducing it as a valuable gem of antiquity, in the 12th note to the first Canto of Marmion, published in the beginning of 1808, as furnished by his *'friend and correspondent, Robert Surtees Esq. of Mainsforth'.*

Yet all this was a mere figment of Surtees's imagination, originating in some whim of ascertaining how far he could identify himself with the stirring times, scenes and poetical compositions, which his fancy delighted to dwell on, and which fooled the great Walter Scott. Surtees had wished to have the success of the attempt tested by the unbiased opinion of the very first and best authority on the subject, and the result must have gratified him. The ballad of the 'Death of Featherstone Haugh' retains its place (vollp.240) with the same expressions of obligation to Mr. Surtees for the communication of it, and the same commendation of his teamed proofs of its authenticity. Surtees sent a letter to Scott on December 8th 1806 paying Scott a compliment, regarding the loyalty and spirit of the Clans, to which Scott replied on 17th December, 1806, from Edinburgh part of it as follows describing his own family involvement in border feuds.

"You flatter me very much by pointing out to my attention the feuds of 1715-1745; the truth is that the subject has often and deeply interested me from my earliest youth. My Great grandfather was out, as the phase goes, in Dundee's wars and in 1715 had nearly the honour to be hanged for his pains, had it not been for the interest of Duchess Ann of Buccleuch and Monmouth, to whom I have attempted, [post lorigo intervallo], to pay a debt of gratitude. But besides this my father, although a borderer, transacted business for many Highland Lairds, and particularly for one old man, called Stuart of Invernahyle, who

*had been out in both 1715-1748 and who's tales were the absolute delight of my
childhood. I became a valiant Jackobite at that age, often and I have never
quite got rid of the impression, which the 'gallantry,' of Prince Charles made
of my imagination, and I will preserve these stories.*

Surtees was extremely busy with his History of Durham project. Alone in the
mornings, he spent time in the woods and riding through the green lanes or at his
favourite Lough bank, which was beautifully covered with every shade of
Columbine from seed scattered by him when he was a boy. He had pleasure
raising flowers on a garden wall and passers by would often see the Squire
mounted on a short ladder weeding the rough grass from wild pinks and
stonecrop.

When literary friends were with him they made excursions for
information for his History, people said it was extremely interesting being in his
company as he was a great admirer of nature. He studied at length the rise and
fall of families of the county; old gable-end properties or dried up fish ponds; a
Spanish chestnut tree; the green inheritance of the Conyers, and the circling Tees
– full of fish. His thoughts were often on the rising of the north where he often
said many Durham families cruelly and severely suffered because of the
rebellion, especially at the cruel hands of George Bowes, Knight Marshal, he was
equal to any Duke of Alva that ever existed. Surtees thought that there were
interesting points of English and Scottish history especially through Lord
Strathmore at Streatham Castle. Several Bowes were employed at embassies to
Scotland; they were a family of political skill and were also very courageous.

Around the year 1809 both Walter Scott and Robert Surtees wished to
call on each other in Scotland and Durham. In a letter from Edinburgh, Scott
mentioned the following dated Edinburgh, 4th March 1809:

*I am going to London and if perfectly convenient for you and Mrs. Surtees, I
am desirous to pass a day at Mainsforth upon our road. I say our, because I
believe Mrs. Scott will be my fellow traveller.*

Robert Surtees returned a letter on March 15th 1809,

Mainsforth

Dear Sir,

*We shall be happy to see Mrs. Scott and yourself, here for as long as you can
spare us. If you come by the High North Road, you need not push on to
Rushyferd for us, but may reach us in one nine mile stage from Durham. I
believe most of the drivers know the road; you keep the turnpike to Ferryhill
and then, are only two miles from Mainsforth. If you will inquire at Sam*

Beardsley's, Coach and Horses at Ferryhill on the bank by the roadside, he will take care that there shall be a key lodged for your use of a private road, which is both shorter and better than the public one. If the driver does not know it, anyone will direct you; or if I know your time I would send a person to wait for you.

Surtees and Scott met for the first and last time as Scott was living in turmoil of engagements and was frequently obliged to disappoint, but their correspondence and joint research of border conflicts and ballads was stronger than ever. In 1815 Mr. Surtees suffered one of his worst downturns when miss Emma Robinson died. She was sister to Mrs. Surtees and only twenty-one years of age, she died 16th June 1815. He well remembered the date when writing the following lines.

But June is, for a reason dear;
The heaviest month of all the year!
And better suits with me;
November's wild and howling blast;
That only raves of pleasures past;
And shakes the leafless tree

In 1816 appeared the first volume of the History of the County of Durham; the second and third were published in 1829 and 1823. Surtees initially suffered great loss when sending volumes of his 'History' as presents; there were thirteen of the large paper copies and seven of the smaller, distributed as presents. One in particular was sent to John Goodchild of Bishop Wearmouth in April 1818. Goodchild had been a senior partner in a bank that had failed and he replied to Surtees as follows.

My Dear Sir,
I hardly know how to express my feelings on seeing the very handsome present made me of your History of Durham. "Since my misfortunes, I had given up every idea of being in possession of so valuable a work; think then what my feelings must have been on finding it presented to me by you. I shall ever hold it in high estimation; not only as to its real value, but as a proof of your feelings towards me. I was in high hopes I might have seen you at Durham this last week, and could I have spared time, I would of walked to Mainsforth, and paid my compliments, I beg my best wishes and respects to Mrs. Surtees; and wishing you every happiness",
I am dear sir, your much obliged, and very faithful servant
John Goodchild.

The fourth volume, although well advanced was not completed at the time of the author's death. There was a mass of materials although not as yet in order and it was hoped that it did not remain as an unfinished monument to the honour of the county. Parts of the Darlington area were unexplored by Surtees although much documentation and oral information had been collected. Happily the Rev. James Raine, who for years had been a very close friend to Robert and a valued contributor, in that he was very much responsible for the whole design, The fourth volume was published in 1840 in its imperfect state, with the exception of a few pages, for which copy was in the hands of the printers. The whole of it had been printed off under the superintendence of its author. The Author at all times was able to rely on Rev. James Raine with his unwearied zeal and energy. Mr. Raine laboured without remuneration and suffered great loss to complete Surtees's History.

Surtees was kindness itself to animals, he never sold his old horses, taking off their shoes and letting them loose in a good pasture and letting them die in peace. One summer evening while out walking at Mainsforth, he saw an old pony in great distress with pain. Surtees had the pony taken to a stable, but it got steadily worse and its body began to swell. Rev. Raine said, "If that was my pony I would do it an act of kindness and shoot it. "Would you", said Surtees, "then it will be done" Surtees came to the same conclusion and the pony was at peace within five minutes, Surtees would not act on his own in cases such as this, even a worm or fly if he could help in any way, he would. Surtees once kept a number of sheep for his own use but had to give the idea up as he got attached to the sheep and hated taking their lives. His love for dogs was extraordinary, not only his own but those of other peoples. At breakfast he was always surrounded by his pointers and greyhounds, dogs came from near and far to be fed. When losing a dog he felt it tremendously as his words show.

Beneath no high Historic stone,
Tho nobly born, is Carlo laid,
His couch the grass-green turf alone,
And o'er him waves the walnut shade.

Within this still, sequestered garth,
Henceforth shall be his lowly cell;
No more to see the blazing hearth,
No more to range the woodland dell.

Dear, lost companion! Memory oft
Shall bring old Carlo to my view,
And paint, in colours dim and soft,
The lov'd the lost, the kind, the true!

118

Green Erin gave him gentle birth;
O'er lilied France in youth he strayed
Four summers suns; in English earth
He sleeps, beneath the walnut shade

Surtees connected his beloved Mainsforth with a Danish encampment that had left its name, Gormundas, with the hamlet of Garmonsway nearby. His love for antiquities urged him to look for historical connections, especially with things close to his heart. There was known to be a large cavity at Mainsforth known as "The Danes Hole" Another branch of the Surtees family based at Redworth; about a mile to the west of Heighington is a mount called Shackleton on which Crozier Surtees constructed a pleasure house, built round three distinct terraces and is thought to be the remains of a Danish Fort.

Surtees also mentions Winston at this time, saying, '. The Church is a small fabric, chiefly of the early English character. Venerable Elms beneath whose branches a noble prospect of Raby opens to the north shade the Churchyard. There are rich and soft views of the tees, the river washes the foot of the steep wooded bank and forms a long silvery canal until it is lost amongst the woods and cliffs of Selaby and Gainford. The wild Richmondshire Hills bounds the horizon to the south and west. It has been said that a Rector of Winston should never offer to a lady who had not seen at this enchanted spot, as he could never be sure that she did not marry the situation. The beauties of wood and vale and water, gives a gentle and honourable feeling of content and independence.'

As time went on Surtees did not stray too far away without his beloved wife Annie. On one occasion, on leaving Mrs. Surtees at home, he returned quickly recording, "I got home without rain, and my spirits recovered wonderfully as soon as I saw Lough-Bank wood; I found all well and invited myself to dine on a roast chicken; a red herring; and a moderate glass of old Madeira. It is nice to see green fields again; Red Beech and Brown Oaks". When on a few days absence at York where he had fatigued himself on documentary researches he writes to Mrs. Surtees *"I will promise you not to tire myself again, and to rest like a decent Christian on Sunday. I rest in hope to see you soon, which I most earnestly long and desire. I am at times very home sick".*

Visits to Scotland

In the year 1803 Surtees made a tour to Scotland with his College friend Sir Wastell Brisco of Crofton halt, Cumberland. The route taken by them was according to notes kept by Surtees.

Auckland; Wolsingham; Hexham; Rothbury; Alnwick; Chillingham; Wark; Kelso; Dryburgh; Melrose; Dalkieth; Edinburgh; Perth; Dundee; Glamis; Dunkeld; Blair; Athol; Loch-lomond; Glasgow; and Lanark, returning through

Cumberland and Westmorland; Greta Bridge; and Richmond. A few observations recorded by Surtees were as follows.

Wolsingham

Stone plentiful, Church Yard filled with monuments originating from respectable families from 1600.

Cold Rowley

Descending into a beautiful vale to the river Derwant, abounding in waterfalls fringed with woodland.

Chillington Castle.

The castle unspoilt by the hand of modern elegance, the residence of the martial family of Grey, guardians of the borders.

Rothbury

Resorted to during the summer and autumn months by invalids for the goat's milk and pure air, Thrumb (a remarkable Waterfall) and a walk by the Coquet mollifies the heart of many a Barbara Allen.

Second Visit to Scotland

In the summer of 1819 Surtees and Mr. Raine had to make a visit to Scotland, visiting Abbottsford going by way of Coldingham. In Edinburgh Surtees was especially interested in "Grey Friars" churchyard and the perishing tombs of the martyred Covenanters. He visited the Church Yard often, discussing their history. Surtees met for the first time the celebrated Scottish poet James Hogg. Surtees and Raine stayed at Walkers Hotel in Princess Street, where Hogg visited them regularly. Surtees and Hogg walking hand in hand, as was the custom, deep in conversation of Scottish History, and legendary lore. Surtees contacted his friend Walter (now Sir Walter). He asked that he might have a flying visit to Abbotsford, to see him. Scott replying that he would be glad to see him, adding that he had recently been ill, but saying he was better now and was using Calomel for prevention sake.

Surtees and Raine met up with Scott when they were like two brothers and immediately in deep conversation on Border History and Border Ballads. On the road to Edinburgh, Surtees had noted a newly published book, written by Scott 'Wolfs Crag', to that point authorship was secret but Surtees was aware that Scott was the author. A print of the battle of Otterburn, which was hung in Scott's dining room, interested Surtees a great deal, but in a short time the two men were in deep conversation on Douglas and Percy, and the chivalry of old. The flashes of genius from the two men were amazing. Scott listened to Surtees with profound attention and, according to Raine; Surtees was at his very best. Dinner was served with Scott at the head of the table; a piper was in attendance and nearly deafened them. Surtees attempted to give the piper money but he quickly refused it, accepting only when Scott told him that he was a great friend of the house.

Third Visit to Scotland

The Publishing of the second and third volumes of the history of Durham was progressing well and in the the year 1823 Surtees and his wife decided to take a holiday to Scotland, not for research but as a well earned rest visiting romantic places of note, Walter Scott advising them on the best route as follows: Bothwell Castle; Hamilton; Lanark; Stonbyres Fall; Cartland Craigs [an astonishing Glen]; leaving the carriage to walk to Baroald. On the second day Scott advised as follows: Bigger; Peebles Melrose; Elebank Tower; Ashsteel; Clovenford; Selkirk; Yair; rivers Tweed and Ettrick; Abbotsford; Melrose. Sir Walter Scott wished them a pleasant journey and fine weather.

It's Sad to Die in spring:

Robert Surtees had never been a man of good health, he was now finding he was having a constitutional failure. After a visit to his mother-in-law and great friend, Mrs. Robinson, at Hendon, Sunderland, he spoke to his wife who met him on the terrace, where he appeared to have a cold. He had ridden from Durham to Ferryhill on the outside of a coach; this was on Monday 27th January 1834. Later in the week he complained of a pain in the side, when they sent for the family surgeon who administered medicine and leeches. Inflammation rapidly advanced and Doctor Brown of Sunderland was called, with no further medication. Surtees visited his library with his wife which would be the second last visit saying to his wife "Annie, I shall never be here again, these books will be yours. She replied, "So they may be Surtees, and I would never like to part with them, but don't you think it would be well to send your manuscripts to some public Library, where they would be of some use? It was later found that from most letters sent to Surtees, by Sir Walter Scott, the signatures had been removed, as, at the time Scott had a great following, not only in Scotland but also in England; he agreed with Annie saying he would make a selection in a day or two please God. Shortly after he was laid up in his sick bed. A bright sun reminded him of his favourite time of the year and he said, "I shall never more see the peach-blossoms, or the flowers of spring. It's hard to die in spring," and he thought of his favourite Layden's lines...

'But sad is he that dies in spring,
When flowers begin to blow,
and larks to sing,
and makes it doubly hard with life to part'

It had been his constant morning custom to watch the blossoms as they came out, and the first was usually laid on the breakfast table where he breakfasted with friends. 'God', had placed him in paradise where he had everything to make him happy. As death neared he met it with composure, gratitude, and resignation to the One whose beneficence had given and whose pleasure it was to take a way. His mind had always been happy in never feeling a shadow of doubt on the truth of Revelation; and he felt, in the hour of trial, the blessedness of that faith which through life he had possessed; nor had his faith been a mere general acquiescence. He was a constant attendant on public worship and family prayer; seldom a day passed without his little green testament being in use. About two-o-clock on Friday morning, February 7th, he said to Mrs. Surtees "Annie, I am very ill. I should have liked to receive the Sacrament, but I am too ill now to send for anyone, but I give it to myself. Don't make yourself uneasy as to my state. I think as deeply as a man can think. You know I am blessed in the power of memory and use it in repeating things to myself, Poor Bradley, he won't like to dig my grave...he knows where I wish to be buried. I pity your mother most, she is an old woman, and has had many sorrows; and she has loved me as I have loved her. I have left you for your life every sixpence that I possess and I hope the sun will go down brightly shining on your latter days."

About two o clock on the mournful day he died February 11th, he called Mrs. Surtees to the bedside and said, "Annie, I am dead", the answer he heard was a prayer that he might sleep in Jesus. Affection was strong in death; on the 15th He was carried to that grave which 'poor Bradley' had dug deep in the rock that forms the brow of the hill on the south side of Bishop Middleham Church yard. Robert was buried close to his brother in law, Marshal Robinson Esq., and Marianne Page, the niece of his wife, who died at school in Durham. He had a great regard to both and could be seen often-placing flowers on their graves. In the Chancel of Bishop Middleham Church a monument was erected carved in Roche Abbey stone, the design of which was presented to Mrs. Surtees by Mr. Blore who's talents have contributed so much to the establishment of the History of Durham. On the marble tablet is the following inscription.

Robert Surtees
Of Mainsforth Esq., M.A. & F.S.A.
The only son of Robert and Dorothy Surtees,
And the author of the History and Antiquities of The County Palatine of Durham,
Was born on the first day of April 1779, and
Died on the eleventh day of February 1834.
He married Anne, third daughter of
Ralph Robinson, of Herrington Esq., and by her
This monument is erected to his memory.
His talents, acquirements, and character
Are developed in his book; and in the memoir
Of his life prefixed to it by a friendly but

Impartial hand. His Christian Faith,
Principles, and hopes are best described in
His own memorable Words:

I am very sensible to the hardness of my heart
And of my totally corrupt nature.
My only hope is in the merits of Christ, but I
Cannot hope for His grace unless I strive to
Obtain it. What is our business? To make our
Election sure—to take heed to our salvation.
Libra nos, Domine Jesu! Audi nos

STOB CROSS
Robert Surtees
Then might the pitying bard the tale repeat,
Of hapless village love in ages past;
How the pale maid, the victim of deceit,
Sunk like the primrose in the Northern blast.

See where the ringdoves haunt yon ruin'd tower,
Where ivy twines amidst the ashen spray;
There still she hovers round the lonely bower,
Where anguish closed her melancholy day.
A dove she seems distinguished from the rest,
Three crimson blood-drops stain her snowy breast.

A few fields to the south of Cornforth stands a ruined dovecote, haunted by a brood of woodpigeons. Here a poor girl put herself down for love, because of her traitor lover, and her spirit still hovers round the cote, in the form of a milk white dove. The deceiver drowned him self some years later in the Float beck, and is buried where the four roads meet with a stob driven through his body, thus calling the area Stob Cross.

Bishop Middle-ham Church:
where Robert Surtees was baptised and buried , infact the whole ***Surtees*** *family are buried here . In the Chancel there is a monument carved in Roche Abbey stone with a dedication to Robert Surtees:*

<u>Mainsforth Hall</u> *in 1920, seat of the* **<u>'Surtees Family'</u>**, *The Hall was re-built in 1725 and was described at the time as a good specimen of an English Mansion. The house was combined with comfort and elegance. The Hall sadly fell into disrepair after the second world war and finally demolished in 1962:*

The only means of transport prior to the 19th. Century was stage Coach. Surtees often used this transport. The travellers endured terrible weather conditions and usually the stage coach carried more than twenty people more outside than in:

BOLCKOW & VAUGHAN
(Middlesbrough Ironmasters)

Henry Bolckow

Bolckow was born to Caroline and Henry Bolckow, at Sulten, Prussia on December 6th 1806, his full name being Henry William Ferdinand Bolckow. Sulten stands near the river Recknitz, the town being situated not far from the Prussian border. Most people in the area were employed in agriculture, mainly in the production of wheat, which was transported via Rostock to the rest of Europe. At the time of his birth, Napoleon with his powerful army, ravished the country. The Balckow family was fairly prosperous and members of the Junker Class (country gentlemen). Henry's father owned a large estate around Sullen. Being fairly prosperous they had their son educated privately, after which he was placed in a merchant's office in Rostock, where it was thought he would have every chance to follow a commercial career befitting for the Bolckow family.

Henry laboured a further six years in this office, learning as much as he could of the corn and agriculture business. Henry made friends with Christian Allhusen, who had a brother in business in Newcastle-upon-Tyne, England, he shortly joined his brother and invited Henry Bolckow to join him in Newcastle, the year was 1827. Bolckow travelled to Newcastle where he began employment as a clerk for C. Allhusen and Compány. In a short time he gained promotion to junior partner, because of his experience and business acumen. The company was involved in the corn trade, as merchants in the Quayside; they also had a granary in Pandon Street. The main object of corn companies at the time was basically speculation, the companies holding back the corn until the prices expanded, with the help of British legislation on the Corn Law.

For twelve years Bolckow remained with this Company and earned himself a fortune of £50,000 with speculative dealings. Bolckow met a lady at this time, Miriam Hay; she was a widow and owned a tobacconist shop on the quayside. This led him to becoming friends with a person who would play a large part in his life. The person's name was John Vaughan; Vaughan was courting Miriam's sister and both men married the sisters, becoming brothers in law

John Vaughan

Vaughan was born on December 21st1799, of Welsh decent. His father was an ironworker in South Wales owned by Mr. Guest. John was a foreman at Dowlais Ironworks in South Wales before moving to Carlisle in 1825. He married at Carlisle, the marriage producing one child, Thomas, who was born there. John Vaughan moved from Carlisle to Walker-on-Tyne in 1832 becoming manager for 'Losh, Wilson & Bell' for the Walker Iron Works. Fate seemed to bring Bolckow and Vaughan together because the two met at the time of courting sisters, and later together, forming a formidable partnership that would completely develop Middlesborough, and indeed, Cleveland, turning it into the Iron Capital of Europe if not the world, employing thousands of people.

Partner

Both enjoyed each other's company, Bolckow being a man of capital, hated the annual fluctuations in the corn trade. In 1839 Henry Bolckow was seeking a new commercial venture, Vaughan with his experience in the iron trade, and knowing the potential growth in the Railways, encouraged Bolckow to invest in Iron. Bolckow was convinced, terminating his partnership with C. Allhusen & Company. Just prior to this termination a meeting had been held at Pilgrim Street, Newcastle upon Tyne, between Joseph Pease, John Vaughan, and Henry Bolckow, after which they were convinced the best commercial venture of the day was indeed iron. Hundreds of miles of rail track would be destined to be laid in England alone; and the coal industry making it all possible in the north of England, when transporting it, sea outlets would be badly needed as production increased, because of the iron trade. Joseph Pease had advised the partners to purchase cheaply six acres of land close to the river Tees; he also provided them with letters of introduction to the coal owners of South Durham. The letter read as follows.

"The Bearer, Mr. John Vaughan, of the firm of Bolckow and Vaughan being about to visit the owners of coal, wishes me to recommend him as likely to become an extensive consumer of coal.

Joseph Pease also believed that without this present interest in iron ore, Middlesborough would not survive economically, and seemed desperate for the partners to develop the area. But it was found that Bolckow and Vaughan, both rational thinkers had fully considered the area for their headquarters, taking into account deeper sea and better facilities for exporting heavy goods. Lastly, they had been guided by James Harris (S & D Engineer) independently, who informed them that Middlesborough was a better prospect than Hartlepool or Stockton and ideally situated for coal from Durham and limestone from Cleveland. The partners started with Ironworks at Middlesborough in 1841 to process pig iron, for rail, bar, and rod. Rails of 73 lb per yard were being rolled for the S & D Railway; this was an example of the support given to the partnership by Joseph Pease who was then the chairman of S & D.

Bolckow & Vaughan lived next door to each other in Cleveland Street, Middlesborough, which is today part of Queens Square; the partners formed an ideal business team, Bolckow a man of capital and Vaughan in iron management. In 1842, an explosion occurred at Vulcan Street when a large boiler burst carrying away the roof of the building. Men were injured and two Irish labourers were literally boiled to death. Three men lost their lives and thirty were injured. By 1846, 20,000 tons of iron was being processed at Vulcan Street, importing the pig iron from Scotland. Bolckow had hopes at the time of being totally self-sufficient, owning: iron mines, railways, ships, blast furnaces, and coalmines. It was a step in this direction when they gained the contract to build engines for '*SS Rose*', which was under construction at Stockton in 1843. It was absolutely essential that adequate supplies of Scottish pig iron were maintained, but during 1845 it fluctuated and rose from £2 to £6 a ton. The partners felt it was important to look for a local supply and this was found as close as Whitby. This decided the partnership decided to erect a number of smelting furnaces at Witton Park, twenty miles to the west of Middlesborough.

Ironstone Discovery

One of the most important days of Cleveland history was 8th June 1850; this was the day an exciting discovery was made by John Vaughan and a geologist, John Marley from Darlington. They found the existence of a bed of ironstone to the south east of Middlesborough. A tramway was built down the side of Eston Hills to a local track, resulting in 4,041 tons of ironstone being transported to Witton Park. The following year a branch railway was added to Middlesborough so that even more iron ore could be taken to Witton. Marley estimated that the partnership needed initially 1000 tons a week, but before the permanent railway had been completed, this figure was increased to 1000 tons a day. The Middlesborough blast furnaces were eventually opened, where Vaughan introduced the Bell and Hopper system invented by Parry, of Ebbw Vale. This allowed the closure of the top of the furnace. This Cleveland iron making practice led the world in the second half of the nineteenth century.

Twenty years before the district of Cleveland was an agricultural centre and of little importance. Thirty years later it had grown from obscurity to a position of renown in the world of the iron trade. The discovery of the Eston ironstone acted as a catalyst and also a stimulus for the future economic expansion of the area. The reason for the newfound wealth was governed by the rise in the fortunes of Bolckow and Vaughan, whose expansion after 1850 was incredible. After the exciting discovery of ironstone at Eston, hopes were high that further ore would be found. Two branch railway lines existed into the ironstone area. One opened by Bolckow & Vaughan to get ironstone from Eston mines, the other from Upleatham and was owned by the Derwant iron Company, who were rivals to the S & D Railway. By now Joseph Pease had his very able son, Joseph Whitwell Pease, to assist him in business and in November 1851 they issued a prospectus for a new Railway Company, which would run from Middlesborough to Guisborough with two branches to the Cleveland Hills. Prior to the newfound wealth with iron ore, the S&D Railway had undergone a downturn and economic difficulties. The present prospectus was seen, as an attempt by the Pease's to monopolise the freight in the new boom area. Many thought that the line was a bad commercial venture, John Vaughan among them, and the subscription list was filled slowly.

The line was completed in 1854, and the Pease's gamble with the line seemed to be paying off, when negotiations were opened with Robert Challenor for permission to survey estates in Guisborough. Permission was granted and iron ore was found in abundance. Later there was wrangling on mining rights, but in February 1855, an agreement between Bolckow and Challoner was made, and signed, granting the iron magnates the ironstone rights of; in, upon, and under lands north of the Middlesborough to Guisborough Railway. They were also granted the rights to sink pits, set up machinery, construct railways, and erect houses, workshops, and offices for agents and engineers, as well as twenty cottages for workmen near to the mines. Challenor retained the rights of any other mineral found on the land. The partnership had to undertake not to destroy fish and game, not to underlet or assign. They also promised not to spoil the scenic beauty of the estate and Challenor could inspect the workings any time.

Bolckow and Vaughan agreed to pay surface rent of not less than £2 per acre and a rent of £300 in the first year, rising to £1000 in the third year and every subsequent year. The agreement held until 1877 when about this time Challenor brought a civil action against Bolckow and the 1855 lease saying they had wrongly deducted property tax. By then general rates and poor rates for the mines had been assessed and Bolckow had rightly deducted these from the rent. He pointed out that royalties and rent were to be paid free of taxes, rates, or impositions laid on the property by Government. Challenor was defeated on his objection locally, when he took it to the House of Lords, he was again defeated. By the date of the action, the Partnership had been transferred into a 'Limited Company' and the action was aimed at the new company. The action showed Bolckow's astuteness in legal matters, later the action did not embitter relations because the lease lasted until 1921 some 66 years. Legally the partnership did not exist until 1865; there is evidence that in reality it came into being in 1853. A verbal agreement existed from the first ever meeting and the partners trusted each other, so much so that a legal agreement was not necessary until 1853, when there was so much litigation and agreements having to be finalised.

Right through his commercial career, Bolckow wished to be self sufficient, at a meeting held in 1865, when he was chairman, he pointed out the advantages of owning ironstone and coal mines, with a limestone supply, along with the process ability. The ten-year period between 1851 and 1861 iron stone production rose from 13,000 tons to 609,000 tons with the proportion of finished products just as significant. The smelting process was commenced at Middlesborough, rivals Elwon and Co. and Messrs. Sherwood, Sydney and Smith were taken over so that by 1861 Bolckow and Vaughan were the largest and wealthiest iron masters. The degree of self-sufficiency could be seen from the diversity of the holdings, before they were transferred to a Limited Company. Hematite mines at Eston, Guisborough, Upsal, and Skelton supplied ore. Coalmines at: White Lee, Woodifield, Shildon, West Auckland and Byers Green, all which had been sunk by the Coulson's, who were sinking one colliery after another at this time; supplied over a million tons of coal each year. Their own quarry at Bishopley supplied limestone. Their own railway to the docks, loaded onto their own ships, with finished products. Ten thousand people were employed and a million pounds paid out in wages, well before 1864 Bolckow had achieved his dream of self-sufficiency. Both partners, by 1864, wished to convert their holdings into a Limited Liability Company mainly to enjoy some of the fruits of their labour. An act had been passed in Parliament in 1862, which absolved shareholders from being personally responsible for company's debts. Accordingly they converted their company at the end of 1864, and on January 1st 1865 they, commenced trading as a limited company, with ten directors, among whom were, Henry Bolckow, John Vaughan, Benjamin Whitworth, (MP for Manchester), and Ald. Pochin (Mayor of Salford), each member having to submit himself for re-election every three years. Henry Bolckow however remained as Chairman until his death in 1878. The annual General Meeting was held at the Memorial Hall, Albert Square, and Manchester in November 1866.

The shares were made up of 25,000 of £100 each, 8000 being held by Bolckow and Vaughan. The subscribed capital being £1.5 million and the paid up capital amounting to £1.2 million. In his report to shareholders Bolckow revealed that their interest in the new company was assessed at being £1.5 million, but the new directors refused to accept this valuation, after which an independent valuation was carried out during 1865, when the purchasing price was fixed at £995,000 and after forwarding some cash to the ex-partnership, the new Company still owed them £280,000 this was to be paid in six half yearly installments. Thus the deficit, which would show on the accounts, left the ex-partners in full control of the company. Henry Bolckow commented that the new company had inherited a valuable property at a very modest price, consisting of three large works; five collieries; and various iron stone mines. All would have to be sold to the new company for about £700,000. Although 1865 was marked by a series of downturns including 10% bank rate and a strike lasting eighteen weeks, and a war on the continent, Bolckow was still able to report a profit of £134,914, which entitled the shareholders to a 10% dividend. As the years progressed the company kept abreast of technology and continued to expand when the original capital rose to £3.5 million, a shining example of a company surviving all kinds of pressures and still making a profit. Bolckow and Vaughan, both had terms representing Middlesborough in politics; Bolckow was Lord Mayor in 1865, where he often entertained dignitaries and public representatives at his residence at Marton Hall. He also represented the town as a Liberal MP in 1874, his hold over the electorate was overwhelming, polling 3719, Kane, (Labour) 1541, Hopkins (Conservative) 996.

Captain Cook Manuscript:

Bolckow, being a Prussian at birth, amassed a vast fortune in England and as such wished to be totally British and give some of his wealth back in the process. As early as 1841 he made numerous attempts to naturalise himself, and he bought Marton Hall to develop an interest in the area around him. Captain Cook was a native of Marton in fact part of Bolckow's estate. Bolckow completely restored Cook's home making it a place of local interest, he had an admiration for Cook and all that he achieved. When anything connected with the great man came up for auction, he was one of the keenest buyers. Over the years he collected important journals and dairies, these had been assumed lost but Bolckow owned them.

In 1868, a group of ten manuscripts were auctioned by Messrs. Puttick and Simpson of 47 Leicester Square, London. (Lot 640) was the most important of the documents, being the Holograph Journal on the charting of New Zealand and Australia between 1769 and 1771. A dealer called Massey sold them to Bolckow, the cost being £14.15. 0. Whatever the motives, the journals ended up in the library at Marton Hall, where they came to light by the trustees of Bolckow's nephew. They came up for auction in May, 1888, at Sotheby's making £71,387, which was for some time a record for sales in one day.

, Bolckow & Vaughan had brought prosperity to Middlesborough and Bolckow wished to give something back to the people of the area who had backed him over the years. Subsequently, in 1868, he bought ninety-seven acres of land for £19,600, to provide a park for the people. He shunned calling the park after himself naming it after the late Prince Consort, 'Albert' who was a Prussian himself. Her Majesty was in full agreement calling the park 'Albert Park'.

Bolckow engaged a well-known landscape, Gardner, from Wakefield, bearing the full cost. Before the park opened the cost had mushroomed to £30,000, paid gladly by Bolckow. At a banquet held at Marton Hall later, the Archbishop of York praised Bolckow tremendously and the press also sang his praises calling him a "Philanthropic Donor"

The End

Throughout 1877, Bolckow suffered with kidney disease, by August the same year his health deteriorated and he was confined to his London Home at 33 Princess Gate. Bolckow's doctor recommended a change of environment and air and in May he went to Ramsgate, where his health improved, but deteriorated again and on Tuesday June 18th 1878, at the Granville Hotel, Ramsgate, Henry Bolckow died. A wish that he be interned at Marton Cemetery was carried out, and a special train brought the coffin and mourners from London to Middlesborough, then by carriage on to Marton Hall on June 22nd. The huge cortege left Marton Hall for the parish church where the Reverend J. K. Bailey conducted the service. Bolckow was buried in a grave overlooking the road and between avenues of lime trees; an inscription on the now neglected tomb reads, *'Blessed are the peacemakers, for they shall be called the children of God'*. A statue of Bolckow now stands in Albert Park; most people when passing daily are quite oblivious to the debt owed to Henry Bolckow.

John Vaughan

Sometime after Vaughan was Mayor in 1858, his health deteriorated and in 1864 he took less interest in the business. His doctors ordered him to go to London in 1867 and he died there on 16th September 1868. In 1879 Joseph Dodd's, MP for Stockton, presented to Middlesborough, on behalf of some subscribers, a portrait of John Vaughan which is in the Council Chamber. A statue of Vaughan was unveiled on 29th September 1884 near the Albert Bridge and was moved to Victoria Square on 23rd October 1904. His son, Thomas, served as Mayor of Middlesborough in 1871 and died in 1900.

Henry William Ferdinand Bolckow :   *John Vaughan:*

Marton Hall; Bolckow's home; below Gunnergate Hall; the home of John Vaughan:

Port Darlington 1830

Above the statue of Bolckow in Exchange Square, Middlesbrough 1986 below John Vaughan in Victoria Square 1906

Name & Place Index

Name & Place Index

Name & Place Index

Name & Place Index

Name & Place Index

Name & Place Index

Name & Place Index

Name & Place Index

Name & Place Index

Name & Place Index

Name & Place Index